Kathy Davis and Scatter Joy are registered trademarks of Kathy Davis Designs, Inc.

Published in Ambler, PA by Scatter Joy Publishing.

Project Editor: Patrick Regan
Creative Director: Kimberly Seslar
Designed by Kathy Davis Studios

ISBN-10: 0-9823259-0-8
ISBN-13: 978-0-9823259-0-2

Library of Congress Control Number: 2009900731

Printed and bound in China

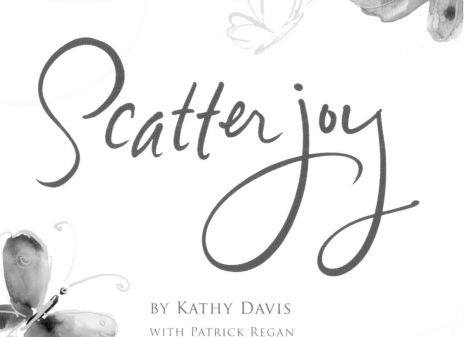

Scatter joy

BY KATHY DAVIS
with PATRICK REGAN

SCATTER JOY
PUBLISHING.

To the many people who served as inspiration for this book and who inspire me day in and day out, I thank you from the bottom of my heart.

To my dear and loving family, who are ever patient with my endless search for joy and meaning; to my faithful and talented team at Kathy Davis Studios; John, Kim, Lorraine, Fred, Jon, Maureen, Melissa, Katie, Tyler, Stephanie, and, especially Janet and Meghann, for their support, insight and contributions.

And, most of all, to the two people who were with me every step of the way while working on this project...

Patrick, my friend, co-writer, and adviser, who gently guided and encouraged me through my muddle...

And Peter, who is my biggest cheerleader, my typist, and my shoulder to lean on...

I couldn't have done it without you, guys. Thank you.

This book is dedicated
to Peter,
who helps me rediscover my joy
when I fail to find it on my own.

TABLE OF CONTENTS

Preface

Sitting down to write a book like this is not easy. At least it wasn't for me. The difficult part wasn't coming up with the personal stories and anecdotes that fill its pages. That was actually kind of fun. The hard part was dealing with a persistent little voice in my head that whispered, "Who are YOU to offer advice on living? What exactly qualifies YOU as an expert?"

My answers to these nagging questions are "Nobody" and "Nothing," respectively. The simple truth is I'm no more qualified than the next person. For this reason, I was hesitant to write a book like this — that is, a book filled with ideas about how readers might build a more joyful life for themselves and for the people that surround them. After all, every person's life journey is unique, and every person's circumstances are different. Who am I to tell anyone else how to be joyful? But, some trusted friends persisted even more than that little voice, and they eventually convinced me that in sharing the story of my personal quest for a more joy-filled life, I might encourage others to find their own path.

Ultimately, though, the main reason I went ahead and wrote this book is because I believe in the Scatter Joy concept. I believe that everyone both craves joy and deserves to have it. And I believe that the world will be a better place if we share our joy with others. If one of my stories or experiences helps inspire even just one person to invite more joy into their life or to share a kindness with another, then this endeavor will have been worth it.

I feel extremely fortunate to have been given the opportunity to share my thoughts, feelings, favorite quotes, and life experiences in the pages of this book. My hope is that it will inspire you, empower you, and stir in you a desire to join this simple movement.

to Scatter Joy

All My Best,
Kathy

An Artist's Journey Toward Joy

Starting Small

As far back as I can remember, I loved making things and playing with crayons, paint, paste—basically, anything that would make a mess! Whether I was truly blessed with an artistic gene or simply responding to the joy I felt while immersed in creative chaos is anyone's guess. As a young child, I may only have been feeding off of the positive reinforcement I received from my grandfather, who lived with us when I was growing up. I proudly recall the time when we sat at our linoleum-topped kitchen table, crayons scattered everywhere, and having him compliment the drawing of a cat that I was working on. The fact that he didn't confuse it for a dog, a skunk, or a vacuum cleaner boosted my morale enough for me to think that I might have some legitimate talent. Funny how confidence comes so easily to kids—and how quickly it can slip away when the insecurities of adolescence creep in....

To my child's mind, creation and play were one and the same, and I played my days away making valentines and Christmas ornaments, hand painting Easter eggs, and creating little chicks out of yarn. When not wrapped up in the "holiday rush," I kept equally busy writing and illustrating my own stories and crafting paper dolls. My little neighborhood was a breeding ground for creativity. My friends and I were always busy coordinating "talent" shows, fairs, Halloween festivities, and even a short-lived neighborhood newspaper. Not much news on Lower State Road.

The highlight of elementary school was art class. I remember the art teacher traveling room-to-room, pushing a cart filled with paints, brushes, papers, and fun projects for us to work on. The squeak of that cart's wheels was music to my ears!

As a child I never had special training in art. In fact, the only formal lessons I ever took were for baton twirling—a skill which, sadly, has little application in the adult world. And while I certainly would have enjoyed taking dance lessons or art instruction,

2nd grade

14

my upbringing was pretty simple. I came from a very modest, middle-class family. The fact that I even had baton lessons made me feel like a pretty lucky kid!

So, throughout school, I always relished my art classes. In fact, when I got to high school, I chose a basic studies course over the college-prep curriculum just so I could fit in an art class. That decision hinted at my passion, yet my full-blown commitment to art was still many years away.

DEALING WITH DOUBT

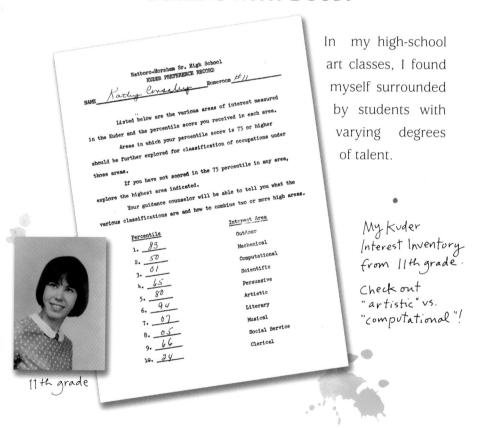

In my high-school art classes, I found myself surrounded by students with varying degrees of talent.

Hatboro-Horsham Sr. High School
KUDER PREFERENCE RECORD

NAME Kathy Crossley   Homeroom #11

Listed below are the various areas of interest measured in the Kuder and the percentile score you received in each area. Areas in which your percentile score is 75 or higher should be further explored for classification of occupations under those areas.

If you have not scored in the 75 percentile in any area, explore the highest area indicated.

Your guidance counselor will be able to tell you what the various classifications are and how to combine two or more high areas.

Percentile	Interest Area
1. 83	Outdoor
2. 50	Mechanical
3. 01	Computational
4. 65	Scientific
5. 80	Persuasive
6. 94	Artistic
7. 67	Literary
8. 05	Musical
9. 66	Social Service
10. 24	Clerical

My Kuder
Interest Inventory
from 11th grade.

Check out
"artistic" vs.
"computational"!

11th grade

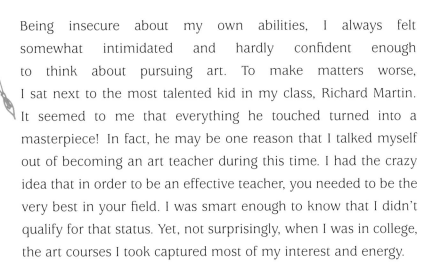

Being insecure about my own abilities, I always felt somewhat intimidated and hardly confident enough to think about pursuing art. To make matters worse, I sat next to the most talented kid in my class, Richard Martin. It seemed to me that everything he touched turned into a masterpiece! In fact, he may be one reason that I talked myself out of becoming an art teacher during this time. I had the crazy idea that in order to be an effective teacher, you needed to be the very best in your field. I was smart enough to know that I didn't qualify for that status. Yet, not surprisingly, when I was in college, the art courses I took captured most of my interest and energy.

Thinking about those years now, I realize that my passion may have been less about art and more about being creative. Today, while I don't consider myself an accomplished artist… or writer… or CEO, for that matter, I see myself primarily as a choreographer of sorts. In both my artwork and my business, what's key for me is the way I combine my skills and interests, piecing them together into a form that feels right to me. I needed to find an area that interested me and then find the confidence to pursue it with my whole heart.

Pursuing an interest with your whole heart might sound easy and natural enough, but for me it can be very scary—and I suspect that's true for a lot of people. Wholeheartedly pursuing something involves making a commitment, and it almost always means closing the door to other options. *Putting yourself out there* is the phrase that, for me, describes the vulnerable feeling that comes with taking a creative risk, and over the years I've tried to get comfortable with that very feeling.

Ever since I was a kid, I've enjoyed being involved in a great variety of activities. Interested in so many creative pursuits, I came to think of myself as a jack-of-all-trades and master of none. And while there's nothing wrong with broad-ranging interests, I eventually realized that I was using my self-applied jack-of-all-trades label as an excuse for not committing myself to any one pursuit.

I settled on teaching not because of a strong vocational calling, but because I could imagine myself being a teacher more easily than I could picture myself being a nurse, or a secretary, or... an artist. Furthermore, teaching is a noble profession, and the best teachers find endless ways to bring creativity to the classroom. But would teaching feed my adventurous, entrepreneurial streak? I wasn't sure, but I was excited about using my creative skills in the classroom to inspire children to learn.

I taught elementary school for six years and have no regrets. But after teaching sixth-grade English and science, I decided that if I were going to stick with teaching, I should teach something that I really loved. And I knew in my heart just what that was: art.

6th-Grade teacher
" Miss Consaley "...
soon to become "Mrs. Davis "

Following My Instincts

I had married one of my fellow teachers, and after a year or so was in a position to take a year's leave of absence and go back to school for certification to teach art and for a master's degree in art education. I especially loved my painting and printmaking projects. I was *putting myself out there*—and experiencing the rewards.

After graduate school, I was fortunate to find a job teaching art in—of all places—my former high school! I taught art at the high-school level for two years, and during that time my passion for art deepened. It was truly rewarding to help these young people develop their talents, but I discovered a growing desire to develop my own skills and creative ideas. I began wishing I were one of the students instead of their teacher.

THE GREATEST MISTAKE YOU CAN MAKE IN LIFE IS TO BE CONTINUALLY FEARING YOU WILL MAKE ONE.

ELBERT HUBBARD

At that point, my husband and I had decided to start a family, and as I planned for the birth of my son, I knew I wanted to spend some time at home, focused on being a mom. I promised myself that if, someday, I returned to work full-time, I would find a path to explore my creativity in my own way—though I had no clue as to what direction that would take.

During my years as a new mom, Ben and then his sister, Katie, born a few years later, were the center of my life and a source of genuine joy. I had hoped to spend some free time painting, since I had enjoyed it so much in graduate school, but I found that the little time I had to work on my art was not conducive to doing large paintings. So instead—adjusting to the reality of my situation—I decided to take a calligraphy class at a local art center. These calligraphy workshops became a source of creative enjoyment during those years when I had young ones at home. I eventually began teaching adult classes in the evening, and these were fun times for me. In addition to meeting many fascinating people, I started producing my own cards and projects with my calligraphy and painting.

an early handmade Christmas card

Each year I crafted a Christmas card from our family and got a lot of enjoyment out of that. Just as gratifying was the positive response I got from the people who received them.

Practicing my calligraphy

Before long, I was doing freelance projects from my home. I first volunteered to hand-letter programs for church and create posters for various fundraisers. Then I got some jobs designing wedding invitations, restaurant menus, and logos. Slowly, but surely, I was *putting myself out there*. While I was uncertain about what I was doing, I did find it exciting, and I enjoyed working as my own boss.

I also found in my artwork some escape from a painful situation in my personal life. My marriage had not been working for some time, and freelancing was a way for me to find some independence during this period. My relationship with my husband had become more about being parents together than anything else. We sought counseling, and although we were not able to save our marriage, I did learn a lot of important truths about myself and valuable lessons for life. During this painful time, for instance, I realized that, for too long, I had been making decisions based on what I felt others wanted or needed me to do. At the time, I didn't realize how unhealthy such codependent behavior was. I gradually saw that my people-pleasing tendency was a mask for the insecurity I had about my own decision making.

As difficult as it was to reach this decision, my first marriage ended, and the most heart-wrenching aspect of the divorce was the pain it caused our family. My ex-husband and I were both devoted to our two young children, and putting them through this life-altering experience completely tore us up. Furthermore, no one in my family had ever gone through a divorce. It was not a "first" I was proud of, and my parents were heartbroken over my broken family. But during this tumultuous time when joy was sparse, I found strength in my faith and strength in myself that I didn't know I had. I came to know myself better, and I began to recognize a passion that had been building inside me for years—a passion to free some of my creative and entrepreneurial urges.

This transitional period in my life was certainly painful, but my ex- and I weathered this tough time. Both of us have remained devoted to our kids, and each of us has been a constant presence in their lives. In addition, we have been able to establish a solid friendship in the years since.

SEARCHING WITHIN

When my husband and I separated, however, the financial reality hit: I needed to work full-time again. Everyone naturally assumed I would return to teaching, but in my heart I knew I needed to explore a new direction if I was going to create a life I loved. It was time I followed my heart wherever it might lead. The problem—and the thrill too—was not knowing exactly what that destination might be.

YOU CAN'T CROSS THE SEAS MERELY BY STANDING AND STARING AT THE WATER.

RABINDRANATH TAGORE

So, rather than look for employment in public education, I decided to piece together a living by doing several different part-time jobs. My family thought I was a touch crazy, but I felt that trying my hand at a few different things might help me find a rewarding career, one that would bring me joy.

I continued teaching my adult classes in the evening, and I took a part-time position at a printing company where I began learning about graphic design. I also continued marketing my calligraphy skills on a freelance basis. My life was a real juggling act, especially when I was shuttling my kids to day care and preschool, but I was learning more about myself each day.

our little family

At the printing company, deadlines came fast and furiously. At times, it felt like a pressure cooker, but I learned to keep it together when the heat was on and to not take things too personally. I had all types of responsibilities, including designing business cards, annual reports, and brochures. But the most important lesson I learned at this job was what I *didn't* want to be doing. While these design assignments involved some degree of creativity, they were often frustrating for me because I had to follow strict direction about what the customer wanted. While I was developing some skills that would later serve me well, I also learned that I needed more creative freedom in a career. *So now what?* I asked myself.

My parents always stood ready to help me and their only grandchildren, but I'm sure they would have felt better if I had taken a secure job rather than try to piece together a living with multiple part-time jobs while I tried to find my own path. During this period, my close friends helped me stay optimistic and hopeful. Lorraine, Kathy, and Ursula all urged me on when my courage waned.

TAKING THE LEAP

Ursula helped pitch in with my kids, who adored her, and she also helped build my confidence while I continued to search for an avenue that would both fulfill my needs for creative freedom and enable me to make a good living. Knowing that I enjoyed making my own greeting cards, she urged me to look into the stationery industry. At Ursula's urging, I decided to find out what this world was all about. She and I went to my first trade show, the National Stationery Show at the Jacob Javits Center in New York City.

Walking the aisles of the show, I was completely overwhelmed. In row after row after row of booths, countless companies were displaying their products, all created by talented artists and writers. I was amazed and impressed by all the variety, the colors, the creativity. I started to panic. Why in the world did I think I might be able to compete in this world? Even though I liked making my family's Christmas cards, competing in this big pool of talent was more than I felt prepared for. I felt like a country bumpkin coming into the big city. I was instantly back in that high-school art class, intimidated by the talent sitting next to me.

After I came home, however, a desire began building in me. While intimidated by what I saw, I was excited by it too. *What a fun way to make a living,* I thought. *Why should I let others have all the fun?* The realization hit me that if I was really going to create something rewarding and meaningful for myself, I needed to face my fears: I needed to *put myself out there.*

By the next day, I was ready. I pulled together some of my own work so I could return to the show before it ended its five-day run. I found that an empty Godiva chocolate box was the perfect size for carrying greeting cards. This would be my "portfolio." Deciding to concentrate on a new cut-paper look I had been experimenting with, I quickly assembled a few designs. At the bottom of the box, I placed a small painting I had just finished: a watercolor of an apple blossom from my tree in the backyard. Then, in an act of utter optimism, I made some business cards by hand, each one different, with hand lettering and collaged cutouts of brightly colored paper. I tucked my goods into my chocolate box, secured the lid with a rubber band, and drove the two hours back to New York.

I was a little unsure of myself, but pretty high on adrenaline. Despite suffering the "Imposter Syndrome"[1] the whole time, I somehow found the nerve to walk into this show and through its endless aisles. To my surprise, I met some very encouraging art directors, who supplied me with their artists' guidelines and invited me to send in my work. There were no guarantees, but I left with enough potential leads to have my head spinning! My handmade business cards had been a hit, too. But it was my watercolor apple blossom that seemed to get the best response. I realized I'd better go out and buy some more watercolor paints!

Buoyed by the feedback I got at that show, I drove home more determined than ever to make something of this passion of mine. I read every book on greeting cards I could get my hands on. I began creating cards in any time I could find. I sent my designs into several companies and, little by little, got word that they were going to test my work in the market. I was further amazed by the positive results of these tests. One card at a time, I started to build my little business...and my confidence.

Working my part-time jobs and being a single mom, however, gave me little time to really focus on my new pursuit. The need to make ends meet was an ever-present and worrisome reality. One day I stopped at the store to buy some milk and toilet paper. When I didn't even have enough money in my wallet to pay for those essentials, I felt as if I'd hit rock bottom—and I promised myself then and there that I would do everything I could to avoid this kind of hand-to-mouth existence. But the most difficult realization was when I faced the inevitable decision to sell the house where I had raised my children. Mounting bills and the need for a new roof pushed me over the edge.

When my husband and I divorced, I had vowed to myself that I would keep the house. To me, it meant security and continuity and normalcy. But paying for the house just wasn't realistic anymore. Keeping my home for my kids and myself had seemed so important earlier, but I realized I needed to let go of that idea. After all, the house was not the source of our happiness or security, and the time I spent caring for and worrying about the house was time and energy I was taking away from my kids *and* my new dreams. I made the difficult decision to downsize and buy a small townhouse for the three of us. This letting go enabled me to make ends meet and it gave us a fresh start. It was a relief to live in a new home that required no repairs or outdoor maintenance. I was freer to focus on my children and the new career I hoped to build.

One of the first things I did after we settled into our new home was set up a drawing table in the corner of my bedroom. Sitting at that small table, I started playing with paint and images, and later I moved on to words…and it was like the dike broke. I turned out image after image. I clearly remember one day when my

parents stopped by to visit. The floor was literally littered with small paintings. In amazement, and with a bit of apprehension, my dad asked, "Are you starting to run out of ideas?" Not even close! Somehow the more artwork I did, the more ideas I got. I guess this happens when you finally take the leap and start doing what you were meant to do all along!

I'M on FIRe

But as exhilarating as it was, the journey was also tiring, and the rejections kept pace with the successes. On low days, I would wonder just what I was trying to prove. The old self-doubt would creep in again. Then one spring afternoon the phone rang. A company on the West Coast called to request not one, but *six* greeting cards! They said they really liked my style and hoped to work with me more!

Yippee!!

This order for six cards was the godsend I'd been praying for. I got out my calculator and figured out how many hours I'd have to work at the printing company to make the same amount of money my six-card order was going to pay. Stepping out in blind faith and, finally some self-confidence, I figured I could finally give notice at the printing company. I'll never forget that day: June 8, 1990—my own personal Independence Day.

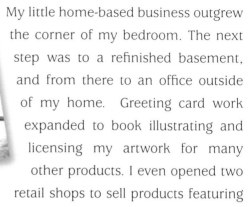

My little home-based business outgrew the corner of my bedroom. The next step was to a refinished basement, and from there to an office outside of my home. Greeting card work expanded to book illustrating and licensing my artwork for many other products. I even opened two retail shops to sell products featuring my artwork—but decided to close them so I could concentrate on my design business. And when I least expected it, I was lucky to meet my future (and current) husband, Peter, while working on my first book. We've been happily married since 1995.

There were many ups and downs through the years as my business grew, but through them all, the one constant has been the tremendous and loyal help I've received from friends, family members, and a dedicated staff. Today I feel just as excited about what I am doing as I did on that June day in 1990.

I COULDN'T
WAIT
~
FOR
S U C C E S S ...
SO
I WENT AHEAD
WITHOUT IT.

JONATHAN WINTERS

Seize the Day

National Stationery Show

There are
many people
who come & go in our lives.

A few
touch us
in ways
that change us
forever,
making us better
from knowing them.

You have made a difference
in my life
and for this
I am grateful.

Kathy Davis
AND COMPANY

A Teacher
Takes a Hand Opens a Mind
Touches a Heart

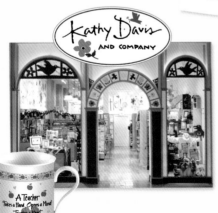

joy

Kathy Davis Designs

Seeds of Kindness

A PROMISE TO KEEP

As my work developed over the years and my business grew, people I worked with started asking about my "brand." I was surprised to learn that I even had a brand, and I certainly didn't know how to describe what it was. But I realized that I needed to be able to describe what I was trying to do if others were to relate and understand. In some companies, this summary of purpose is called a slogan or a mission statement, but I came to think of it as a promise—*a brand promise.*

Wanting to state this promise as succinctly as possible, we started asking customers, clients, and employees what the Kathy Davis brand meant to them. As we dug deeper and deeper, as we analyzed my art and tried to come up with a slogan that distilled all of this information, I got more and more frustrated. Then one day in a meeting, I heard myself say in exasperation, "All I really want to do is scatter joy!" Everyone in the room stopped, and someone said, "You may be on to something!" Scatter Joy has been my mantra—and my brand promise—since that moment.

I can't take the credit for the phrase *scatter joy*. These two words are excerpted from a longer quotation that I came across many years ago while working on a poster design. The quote, by Ralph Waldo Emerson, had a powerful effect on me the moment I read it:

*There is no beautifier of complexion, or form, or behavior,
like the wish to scatter joy and not pain around us.*

joy is a net of love by which you can catch souls.
mother Teresa. 1910-1997

Time spent laughing is time spent with the gods.
Japanese Proverb.

One joy scatters a hundred griefs.
chinese Proverb.

If you tickle yourself, you can laugh when you like.
chinese Proverb.

Scatter joy
Ralph Waldo Emerson 1803-1882

Unshared joy is an unlighted candle.
Spanish Proverb.

And we should consider every day lost on which we have not danced at least once.
Friedrich Nietzche. 1844-1900

The simple phrase, *scatter joy,* truly explains what I hope to do with my art. The joy I get from creating is something that I want, in turn, to share with others. And the fact that—whether through a greeting card, book, or some other product—people may, in turn, pass on some of that joy to others inspires me even more!

Once I adopted "Scatter Joy" as my personal and professional motto, my goal became to scatter joy in three different ways—through art, through living, and through giving.

And scattering joy is what this book is all about. Its pages are filled with anecdotes and ideas, inspiration and affirmation. For me, scattering joy begins with art, but you certainly don't need to be an artist to join this movement. In fact, I hope this book helps you find your own personal way of scattering joy and that you find it as rewarding as I find mine.

If you'd like to share the story of a time when you or someone you know "scattered joy," please do so at ✏ scatterjoy.com! We'd love to hear from you—and, with your permission, your story may appear in a future book.

A FINAL THOUGHT

When I look back, I wonder why, as a young adult, I was so fearful of bringing the art out of my heart and into a career. I took a winding path in my career search, yet my love of art always remained with me. I was in my mid-thirties when I finally made my passion for art a part of my daily life.

Paying close attention to those things that bring us joy is critical to creating a life that we love. Whether it's making things, hiking, studying, or working with people…if it feeds our soul, gives us energy, transports us out of time and into a space of flow…we are meant to do *more* of these things. These gifts help make us the unique individuals we are. These gifts energize us, nurture us, and move us to a place where the fullness of our joy spills over to others. I wish I could banish the guilt most of us feel over spending time doing the things we enjoy!

DO
YOU
HAVE
ART
IN YOUR
HEART ?

While traveling out west about ten years ago, my husband and I happened upon a small shop displaying handcrafted items in the window. I spied a hand-stitched heart, with a quotation written above that read, "Do you have art in your heart?" That saying touched something deep inside of me. I had carried my art around inside my heart for many years before I found the courage to free it. Now that it has wings, I am on a joy-filled journey.

Whatever form of art you are carrying in your heart, I encourage you to honor it, nurture it, and share it with others.

IF YOU ARE
CALLED
TO BE A STREET SWEEPER,
SWEEP STREETS AS

MICHELANGELO
PAINTED,

OR BEETHOVEN
COMPOSED MUSIC,

OR SHAKESPEARE
WROTE POETRY.

SWEEP STREETS
SO WELL
THAT ALL THE HOSTS
OF HEAVEN AND EARTH
WILL PAUSE AND SAY,
. . . .
HERE LIVED A STREET SWEEPER
WHO DID HIS JOB WELL.

MARTIN LUTHER KING, JR.

35

THE SCATTER JOY BRAND PROMISE

Scatter Joy defines my mission, my art, and the essence of my brand. As I like to think of it, there are three aspects to my Scatter Joy mission:

JOY THROUGH ART

JOY THROUGH LIVING

JOY THROUGH GIVING

My hope is that, as you read these pages, you will be able to identify with me and with my Scatter Joy mission to find joy through art, living, and giving.

JOY THROUGH ART

Art washes away the dust of everyday life.
Pablo Picasso

Art is a wonderful expression and response to the world around us. It enlightens us, elevates us, educates us, changes us. It can be an emotional expression, a mindful expression, or a physical expression.

Whether we are making art or simply enjoying art and the everyday design that permeates our lives, our awareness is heightened, our experiences are fuller, and our lives are richer.

My hope is to touch others with my art and to inspire the artist within each one of us.

Joy Through Living

Find the beauty and joy in everyday moments.
Anonymous

Our everyday lives can be so hectic and harried, crowded with pressures, deadlines, and overflowing with information. It is so important that we take precious time for ourselves and those we love and that we make our surroundings and the things we use pleasing and beautiful. Such sensual experiences, add quality to our lives.

Through my words, my images, and my designs, I hope to inspire others to create a life they love.

Joy Through Giving

It is in giving that we receive.
St. Francis of Assisi

Nothing fulfills us and makes our lives richer than sharing with others, and in this world of ours there is so much need for more kindness, better communication, empathy, and understanding.

Showing others we care by giving of ourselves, our time, our talents, and our abundance can make all the difference. Giving back—to the earth, to our community, to those in need, and to our loved ones—enriches not only the recipient but us as well.

Whether it's as simple as sending a greeting card or as critical as contributing to a worthy cause, my desire is to inspire others to not only feel the joy of life, but to scatter it and share it with those around them. Like seeds scattered in a garden, simple kindnesses can bloom, grow, and multiply in the most miraculous ways.

WHAT'S THE ART IN YOUR HEART?

Use what talents you possess.
The woods would be very silent
if no birds sang there
except those that sang best.

Henry Van Dyke

It is impossible for me to tell my story without talking

about art. For me, art is both the filter through which I process

what's important to me and the language I use to communicate

those ideas. Art is also the way I make my living.

But this book was not written solely for artists. Far from it!

Let me explain…

I have two fundamental beliefs when it comes to art:

I believe that everyone has some kind of art in his or her heart, and I believe that inspiration to create art surrounds all of us, all the time.

Art and *artist* can be intimidating words, but I don't think they need to be. I invite you to open your mind to a broader definition of the word *art*. Here's an excerpt from the *World Book Dictionary:*

"any form of human activity that is the product of and appeals primarily to the imagination"; "some kind of skill or practical application of skill."[2]

I like those descriptions. And I have yet to meet someone who doesn't have a special skill or knack for something that enriches their lives... something that excites them and enhances their everyday world.

So what is your passion? What art is in your heart? Or, put simply, what's your "thing"?

My brother Fred, following in the footsteps of my dad, expresses his creativity through landscaping. Fred would be the first to say, "I don't have a creative bone in my body." After all, as a finance guy, Fred deals in the absolutes of numbers; he can't creatively stray from the facts. But in the outdoors, Fred blossoms just as his gardens do. From building pergolas and ponds to creating masterpieces in his flower gardens, he becomes a painter with his flowers and foliage.

Fred's wife, Helen, has a real knack for cooking. Embracing the fine art of entertaining, she researches recipes and whips up dinners for hordes of friends and relatives. Believe me, we enjoy every bit of Helen's art… down to the last bite!

Our friend Brian is a native Bermudian with a winning personality whom we met while vacationing there. Brian's hidden talent is his ability to create teeny-tiny kites, the size of a thumbnail! Exactly how he got started on this is a mystery to me, but Brian has achieved a certain status in his homeland. Local newspapers have featured him in articles and photos as they've highlighted his amazing, offbeat talent.

The point of all these examples is this: whether your art is cooking, scrapbooking, or skydiving, it is something that makes you unique. These passions are real gifts, adding enjoyment to life that we would otherwise miss. Not only that, but these passions provide us ways to share our gifts with others. Now that's what I call "scattering joy"!

Indulging our artistic impulses and following our passions can be such a natural act, yet so many people deny themselves the pleasure. Many people simply don't know how to begin. "Where do you get your ideas?" is a question I hear all the time. My answer is always the same: "Look around you!" I honestly believe that, whatever your art, inspiration is everywhere. Nature is one of my favorite sources of inspiration, but music, architecture, books, and many other forms of artistic expression also inspire me.

When I was finishing up my master's degree, I chose to do my thesis on "Everyday Forms of Art in Society." This idea came to me because I felt that too many people think of art as some lofty and often difficult-to-understand masterpiece that belongs in a museum. This topic also dovetailed with my desire, as a teacher, to help my students become more aware of their surroundings, be inspired by their world, and be attuned to the ways they choose to express themselves. So I photographed a series of common items in an attempt to illustrate personal expression as well as our human quest for both function and pleasing form. My subjects included front doors, shoes, and mailboxes—and the mailbox subject matter became my favorite.

Everyone should carefully observe which way his heart draws him, and then choose that way with all his strength.

Hasidic saying.

What a fascinating assortment of mailboxes I found as I scoured the town and countryside! Some were obviously chosen purely for functionality, but I was amazed by some of the personal expression I discovered! There were hand-painted ones, totem poles, birdhouses, and metal sculptures. I became hooked on this scavenger hunt and had fun imagining the lives of the people behind the mailboxes. How inspiring! (As I

42

write this, I am very aware that we have one of the ugliest mailboxes within a hundred miles! I'm embarrassed to say that it is black plastic and that I chose it purely because of its size and shape. I now realize that I might want to rethink the mailbox at the end of our driveway!) This study of mailboxes just goes to show all the things we notice when we're tuned into them.

And what did my study say about art? It reminded me that good design needs to meet the criteria of both form and function. One of the things I love about the Museum of Modern Art is that it displays not only paintings and sculpture, but also some beautifully designed objects, ranging from chairs to can openers.

Whether it is cooking or calligraphy, landscaping or designing chairs, I believe all of us have a duty—if only to ourselves—to nurture the unique interests and exercise the artistic gifts that we are endowed with. Whether we call it our art, our hobby, or just our "thing," our involvement in it is meaningful because it enables us to express who we are. Inspiration, like art, is everywhere, and both can enrich our lives in many ways. All we need to do is open our eyes to it and invite it in.

Something to Think About:

What is the art in your heart? Do you make enough time to express that?

take time
to notice
all the simple beauties.

JOY THROUGH MINDFULNESS

*Teach us... that we may feel
the importance of every day,
of every hour,
as it passes.* — Jane Austen

As easy as it may sound, living in the moment can be tricky. Our minds are so active with a tremendous influx of information every day, our "to do" lists are never-ending, and our tendency to obsess over the past or worry about the future can easily cloud our awareness of the present. Irretrievable moments slip through the hourglass because our minds are elsewhere!

Mindfulness is the practice of being fully in the moment, of being aware and accepting of our experiences as they happen. Being fully present allows us to be more responsive to the circumstances in our lives.

Too often we find ourselves going through our days on autopilot. Of course some of our activities don't require our focus as much as others do, but by being more mindful or aware, we can find ourselves actually deriving more satisfaction from even the rote chores of life, tasks like cooking a meal or mowing the lawn.

Sometimes we miss the moment because we are trying to do too many things at once. Multitasking has become popular, if not seemingly essential, in our fast-paced world. While this efficiency and productivity may sound good, we miss out on life: we aren't giving any one task our full attention as we switch back and forth from one activity to another, juggling multiple demands at once.

If, however, we choose to focus on one project or one conversation at a time, we can give it our best effort—and we can better live in the moment.

This practice of being more fully aware of our world as we go about our daily activities and thus increasing our capacity for enjoying life is something I never thought much about until I read *Plain and Simple: A Woman's Journey to the Amish* by Sue Bender.[3]

This book recounts Sue's experience of living with the Amish and learning to appreciate their quiet and simple ways. What she discovered was the beauty of the everyday rhythms of their world. She also learned simplicity, commitment, and the joy of doing well whatever you do. Living with the Amish taught Sue how satisfying the simple activities in our lives can be when we go about them with mindfulness and reverence.

What an interesting thought! Suddenly I could feel good about doing the dishes. Before, I had resented the time that this chore stole from other more interesting activities. But, just because I learned how good being in the moment can feel even when I'm washing dishes doesn't mean I always remember to live that way!

It takes vigilance for me to stay in this mind-set, but I am always rewarded when I slow myself down and fully participate in the task at hand.

LIFE IS SHORT.

I LIKE TO PAY ATTENTION WHILE I'M GOING THROUGH IT.

VIGGO MORTENSEN

My friend Mary once confided in me about one very troubling aspect that threatened her otherwise healthy and happy marriage to Bill. The issue was Bill's obsessive need to plan ahead. Always concerned with what came next, he couldn't just "be" in the present moment. Even on vacation, Bill was so busy planning the *next* day's activities that he didn't seem to enjoy what they were doing that day. Sometimes, Mary said, while they were on *one* vacation, her husband was focused on where they should go for the *next* one! Bill was definitely missing out on the joy of the present moment, and Mary said she felt lonely much of the time. Bill's mind and attention were always somewhere else.

It has taken time and effort on both Bill and Mary's part to work through this problem. But Bill has become much better at living in the moment. He is now able to derive more satisfaction by being fully aware, and Mary has the partner she was missing.

From time to time all of us slip into a lack of awareness, and we fail to be in the moment. I know, for example, that when my mind is working overtime, I can try hard to read a book, but I'll notice at some point that I have been skimming over words and even turning pages without really paying attention—and I can't recall a darn word I've read! Yes, it takes practice to live in the moment, but developing that ability is well worth the effort.

We all have choices to make each day and every moment. So let's embrace the joy... and share the joy. It's yours and mine for the taking... and for the giving.

Something to Think About:

What things most often distract you and keep you from living in the moment?
What can you do to reduce these distractions?

Practicing the Art of Living in the Moment

Meditation is one way to practice slowing your mind and being fully aware of your breath, your body, and your place in the universe. I've tried meditation on a limited basis and found it to be relaxing, but challenging. It takes practice to keep intruding thoughts at bay!

However we choose to relax, we must learn to relax completely. Relaxation techniques can help us relax our body and, even more difficult and more important, our mind.

Tips to Try

- Use all of your senses when you try to be in the moment. Focus on each one of them in order to heighten your awareness of the present. When we are stressed or preoccupied, our senses become dulled from disuse.

- Take a few minutes each morning to do some gentle stretching. Notice your breathing and get in tune with how each part of your body is feeling as you awaken it with a simple stretch.

- Take advantage of your time—even while you are standing in a line, waiting for an appointment, or sitting in traffic—and tune in to your state of mind and body. Stretch tense muscles, practice meditation, or record whatever is on your mind in a journal or on a recorder.

- Prioritize your efforts. When you feel pulled in many different directions, stop and list all the things demanding your attention. Then decide which ones deserve your immediate attention and which can wait. Don't forget to include some time for yourself. Then you can relax and focus on one activity at a time, knowing that you will get to the other tasks as you can.

- Try some guided meditation. Countless books, recordings, and resources are available on this topic.

One of my favorite books is: *The Art of Doing Nothing: Simple Ways to Make Time for Yourself* by Véronique Vienne[4]. Among the chapters are "The Art of Breathing," "The Art of Napping," "The Art of Tasting," "The Art of Waiting," and "The Art of Bathing." Yummy thoughts, for sure!

Sometimes the smallest blessings bring the greatest joy.

Anonymous

SIMPLE WAYS TO SCATTER JOY

*We can do no great things,
only small things with great love.*
Mother
Teresa

Scattering joy can and should be an uncomplicated and natural act. The simplest pleasures that we enjoy each day, such as a quiet moment with a warm cup of coffee, the beauty of the setting sun, and the peacefulness of a walk on the beach or through the woods are often our life's truest treasures. And sharing these moments with another person is a simple way to scatter joy—and a way that often touches the heart most deeply.

I smile whenever i think of you.

Consider the power of a smile. Have you noticed that when you smile even though you don't really feel like it, that simple act of curving your lips into a happy face can make you feel better? It has even been found that doing so increases endorphins, the "happy juice" in your body. And when you share that smile with others, not only does your smile make them feel good, but it usually causes them to smile back. What a simple gesture with such a powerful cause-and-effect outcome!

A smile, a handshake, and a hug are among the simplest ways to scatter joy. Paying a compliment, calling a friend, and performing an unexpected act of random kindness are also powerful and uncomplicated ways of spreading joy. Let me give you an example from my recent vacation in Mexico when I was truly touched by the kindness shown me by someone I had just met.

My much-anticipated trip was to consist of one week with my family and a second week on my own so that I could begin writing this book. Since I have two young-adult children with jobs, school, and busy lives of their own, this vacation—the first family vacation we had had in some time—took much advance planning. I was extremely excited about spending a week with my husband and the kids in that warm part of the world. The second week was to be a working vacation, a time when I would be detached from everyday urgencies so that I could focus on my writing. While I was very much looking forward to the second week, I knew I would be missing my family, and I was a bit apprehensive about being on my own in a foreign country.

Early in the first week of the trip, I met Silvia, a friendly woman who worked in our hotel. She offered many suggestions about how we might spend our time in her home country. But she became very quiet when she discovered that I would be on my own that second week. Meekly, she asked me, "Will you still be here on the nineteenth?" When I said yes, she astounded me with an invitation to be a guest at her mother's birthday party in a neighboring town. She went on to say how much her mother enjoyed life and how she'd like me to meet her and be a part of their celebration. Silvia's concern for my loneliness was so sweet and so much appreciated that my eyes misted over at her kind gesture. I thanked her even though I wasn't sure I would attend.

This warm invitation, and the many other kindnesses I received while I was in Mexico, took on a whole new level of meaning for me when, a few days into my vacation, I received devastating news from home. Suffice it to say that that unexpected development changed my time away into something completely different from what I had planned. I did not return home immediately, and my days in Mexico were filled with pain and stress. Simple kindnesses can do a lot to help brighten our days at any time, but when a crisis

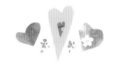

TOO OFTEN WE
UNDERESTIMATE
THE
POWER
OF A TOUCH,
A SMILE,
A KIND WORD,
A LISTENING EAR,
AN HONEST COMPLIMENT,
OR THE SMALLEST
ACT OF CARING,
. . . .
ALL OF WHICH HAVE
THE POTENTIAL
TO TURN A LIFE AROUND.

LEO BUSCAGLIA

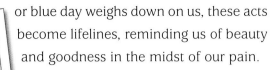

or blue day weighs down on us, these acts become lifelines, reminding us of beauty and goodness in the midst of our pain.

As it turned out, I did accept Silvia's invitation. The warmth and hospitality shown by the twelve party attendees went a long way to help lift my spirits. Only two of the twelve spoke English, and I don't know any Spanish (other than *hola* and *baño*), but smiles and laughter, thank goodness, are universal. For a few hours, I forgot my problems, and I even surprised myself—and delighted my new Mexican "family"—when, blindfolded, I burst open the piñata with a wild swing!

"Look out, piñata!"

That memorable evening, prompted by the unexpected connection of two hearts, went a long way toward turning a depressing week into one marked by some joy. And what prompted it all? Simply a shared smile and a few kind words.

Something to Think About:

Who in your life could use a smile or kind gesture? What can you do for that person?

Joy in the Morning

I have always been delighted
at the prospect of a new day,
a fresh try, one more start,
with perhaps a bit of magic
waiting somewhere behind the morning.

J. B. Priestley

I recall a time in my life when I'd have been the last to consider myself a morning person. I'd sometimes sleep until noon, much as my own twenty-something kids do today. But, as time passed, that pattern gradually changed, as many things do with time. Now I relish the mornings. In fact, morning has become my favorite time of day! There's nothing so pure, quiet, still, and full of hope and promise as those hours before all heck breaks loose!

Joy lives easily and effortlessly in those moments of early light. This is the perfect time of day to make time for yourself—time for meditating, praying, reading, planning, or just plain being. My morning ritual begins with a cup of coffee. (I find most rituals are highly effective when accompanied by a beverage or bite to eat.) This admitted addiction helps jump-start my brain and, just as important, gives me a cup of reassuring warmth to hold close. Bleary-eyed, I then find my way to my comfy, cozy morning chair, located in a spot that catches the first light of day.

Once nestled in, I delve into my word jar. My friend Wendi created this as gift for me. She filled a simple ceramic jar with slips of paper on which she wrote single words. Words such as *hope, transition, courage, beauty,* and *play* lie in wait inside the jar. A couple slips are blank, inviting me to come up with my own word for the day. I shake the jar and then carefully select a word to ponder. Its relevance to what is happening in my life will often surprise me!

After spending a moment with that word and thinking about its significance for my day, I open a small book of readings. I have many such books to choose from, but my favorite is *Peace of Mind* by Amy Dean.[5] Typically, my morning books contain a quotation or passage, followed by some brief words of guidance on the topic, and ending with a parting thought. The readings most often lead me to prayer or meditation.

EVERY DAY IS A
RENEWAL
EVERY MORNING
MIRACLE.
THIS JOY YOU FEE
IS LIFE.

GERTRUDE
STEIN

On busy days this is all I have time for. On other days, I may write in my journal, do a gratitude exercise, or make plans for my day. Once I leave my chair and hit my computer, the e-mail craziness begins, and I slip out of my joyful ritual and confront the urgencies of the day. As we all know, nothing lasts forever. I am just so pleased that I've taken some precious time for myself at the start of a new day. I invite you to do the same.

Something to Think About:

What change(s) can you make in your morning ritual to help start your day off right?

IDEAS FOR FINDING JOY IN THE MORNING

- Try doing some gentle stretching even while you're still in bed.

- Wake up to soft music or nature sounds instead of a blaring alarm. You might even want to get a clock that slowly illuminates to simulate the rising sun.

- Setting the timer on the coffee machine can stir you with the aroma of freshly made brew!

- Try to get up a half hour earlier than the others in your home so you can enjoy some peace in the early part of your day.

- Morning meditation, prayer time, or devotional readings can start you off in the right frame of mind and with the right perspective

- Write in a journal.

- Don't forget that breakfast is the most important meal of the day. Switch it up from the usual cereal or bagel. Fresh fruit, granola, yogurt, and some protein are options that can start you off right.

- Do some morning yoga.

- Exercise in the early hours seems to work best for me - before I'm fully awake and able to rationalize my way out of it!

- Sign up online for a daily e-mail so you will receive an inspiring quote, the news headlines, or cute photos from one of your favorite sites.

Heaven
is
under our feet
as well as
over our heads.

Henry
David
Thoreau

JOY IN THE EVENING

*To me, every hour
of the day and night
is an unspeakably perfect
miracle.* Walt
Whitman

Evening is a natural time for winding down, reflecting, and relaxing after a long day. Early evening hours may be filled with family responsibilities, meetings, classes, activities, or extra work demands. After all that, though, let the evening be an invitation to let go of the stresses of the day. Take some time for yourself so you can prepare for a restful and rejuvenating night's sleep.

Spending a few moments reflecting on the day's activities can help you make the most of your daily experience and prepare you to better face tomorrow. If you are fortunate enough to have your whole family gathered around a dinner table in the evening, seize this perfect opportunity for sharing your stories of the day. When my kids were still at home, my favorite activity around the table was "Best, Worst, Funniest." Each family member takes a turn sharing the high point of the day, the low point of the day, or something that gave them a reason to chuckle. While my request to do this activity usually elicited a groan or two, we learned more about one another with this simple activity than you can imagine.

One year we took a two-week family vacation to Europe, and I recorded in a journal our best, worst, and funniest highlights from each day. Upon returning home, I typed up our journal (this was a real accomplishment for me), inserted photos, and gave a personalized copy to my husband and the kids for Christmas. Mind you, this wasn't a typical vacation activity for me. On most vacations I pretty much collapse, but I am so glad I have those family vacation memories preserved.

Something to Think About:

Do you allow yourself time in the evening to wind down and reflect on your day? What could you do so that you might find that kind of time more often?

IDEAS FOR FINDING JOY IN THE EVENING

- Light a few scented candles.

- Set aside some reading time. Even a few minutes with a good book may help you take your mind off your problems and unwind before you sleep.

- Read to your partner or to your kids. Reading to kids before bedtime will help you form a strong bond with them that never fades.

- Write in a journal. Include thoughts about the day and maybe some hopes for the future. You can also list those aspects or events of the day for which you are especially thankful.

- Watch a favorite show. (If you have TiVo®, record the shows you love and watch them at your leisure—with the added bonus of skipping the commercials!)

- Take a long, hot bath. Light some candles and fill a tub with bubble bath. Luxuriate and unwind in the warm water. Breathe deeply and exhale the cares of the day.

- Practice yoga. Many yoga exercises are best for morning, but some wonderful ones will help you stretch, relax, and unwind before bedtime.

- Call a friend. Share the day's news, frustrations, and highlights—or just enjoy a good chat.

- Treat yourself to a cup of herbal tea and a light snack.

- Listen to some favorite music.

- Go for an evening stroll. Wander through town and look at lights in the windows or walk through a park and listen to the crickets' songs.

- Gaze at the stars.

- Meditate or pray—for guidance, for hope, for rest, for rejuvenation, and for peace—peace in your heart as well as peace in our world.

Mark your days
in ways
that bring
your heart
joy.

Anonymous

JOYS AT WORK

Let us stop equating work
with earning a living,
but rather think of it as an
important component
of making a life.
Ralph C. Weinrich

Our jobs and roles in life undoubtedly vary almost

as much as our fingerprints do, and our experiences at our job

can also vary. Some days can be empowering and fulfilling; other

days can be just plain ol' hard work.

But what if you tend to view your work as drudgery? If, day after

day, you wake up not wanting to go to work, you may want to

reexamine your career choice and look for a position that helps

you feel productive, energized, and rewarded. After all, we spend

more time doing our job than we invest in any other facet of our

> CHOOSE
> A JOB
> YOU LIKE
> &
> YOU WILL
> NEVER
> HAVE TO
> WORK
> A DAY
> IN YOUR
> LIFE.
>
> CONFUCIUS

lives. While making a change can be very difficult and it may even require new training, your efforts to find the right job or career path can make a huge difference in the quality of your life and your joy quotient.

That being said, a job is a job. Even if your work suits your strengths, gives you a sense of accomplishing something worthwhile, and is helping you reach your personal goals, you will have days when you question all of that. Sometimes difficulties with certain projects or certain people, sometimes the repetitive nature of the job or aspects of it that aren't your favorite can get you down.

So how can you deal with all that? You may not be able to control your circumstances, but you can choose to bring some joy into your workday and to share some of that joy with your co-workers.

Something to Think About:

What can you do to make your workplace more joyful?

IDEAS FOR BRINGING JOY TO THE WORKPLACE

- *Snack Attack!* — Food is a great bridge builder and mood enhancer. Share a snack, either fresh-baked or store-bought, with your co-workers. Pick up a box of treats for the workplace while you're on vacation. (We find it impossible to count calories while working at Kathy Davis Studios!)

- *An Apple a Day* — Pack nourishing lunches and snacks to help keep your energy up throughout the day. Carrot sticks, apples, raisins, almonds, trail mix, and cheese and crackers can help you get through your slump times.

- *A Bouquet of Sunshine* — There's nothing like fresh-cut flowers to brighten any workspace and lift people's spirits. Bring in a bouquet from your garden or get a bouquet from my favorite place for flowers, Flowerbud.com. Occasionally spread the sunshine by bringing a fresh flower for the desk of each of your co-workers.

- *Music to My Ears* — Music has been found to improve productivity. If you are in a small office and have a CD player, you may have the option of sharing some of your favorite music with others. At KDS we take turns choosing the music that's played in our common area. One day it may be pop music; on another, it may be oldies, country, or new music, depending on our employees' choices.

- *Give It a Break!* — No matter how responsible and dedicated you are, you need to take breaks periodically. Even five or ten minutes away from your task can rejuvenate you and provide some much needed perspective on your work.

- *Make It Fun!* — In order to get through daunting projects or mundane tasks, make that dreaded job a game. Reward yourself with a snack, a break, or even a piece of gum after you complete small steps as well as big ones.

a KDS outing to local garden "Chanticleer"

- *Expand Your Horizons* — Take advantage of every opportunity for more training or any classes outside of work that may help you do your job with greater expertise or enthusiasm. At KDS, we try to do a monthly or quarterly outing, since inspiration is key to our creative roles. We have visited local gardens, gone to a movie, and attended art shows. Even an hour away from the normal setting can spark new thinking.

- *Scatter Joy* — There's nothing like getting and sending cards or notes of encouragement, congratulations, and friendship. Everyone needs and appreciates words of affirmation or recognition. Even a supportive e-mail or e-card can really brighten someone's day. You might include a favorite quote with every e-mail you send.

Speak to the Earth
and
it shall teach thee.

JOB 12:8

THE JOY OF NATURE

In all things of nature,
there is something of the marvelous.
Aristotle

Nothing inspires me more—both for my art and for my overall sense of well-being—than the infinite beauty of the natural world. Being one with nature soothes my soul and confirms that all is as it should be. At the same time, nature reminds us that there are certain forces bigger than we are and that many things are out of our control. Each of us is just a tiny fragment in this vast universe. This reality both comforts me and inspires me.

Living in the northeastern U.S., we are fortunate to avoid most of nature's fury. Other parts of the world and even other parts of our country are far more prone to hurricanes, tornados, earthquakes, and other natural disasters. My one experience with a significant but not serious earthquake happened during a trip I took to Costa Rica with my brother a couple years ago. What a beautiful part of the world with its rainforests, mountains, coastal splendor—and, as we were about to experience, some occasional seismic activity!

The 6.5 earthquake awakened us from our sleep at 2 a.m. with terrible noise, rattling, shaking, and plaster falling from the ceiling. Our rooms were littered with items that had fallen from cabinets, and power was out all over the area. You haven't seen darkness until you are in the middle of a rainforest at 2 a.m. with no electricity! The aftershocks were almost as strong and as frightening, continuing as they did for another twenty-four hours. Our nerves were frayed. While the damage to the area was minimal—nothing much more than some cracks in the roads and a few collapsed buildings—the whole experience was mind-blowing for me. Talk about feeling tiny in the vastness of the universe!

Mother Nature has definite ways of reminding us that we're not really in control. I have never been in a serious hurricane, but our family visited the ravaged regions of Mississippi and New Orleans to assist with Hurricane Katrina disaster relief. This trip certainly opened our eyes to the power of nature's fury.

The destructive forces of a natural disaster remind us that we need to respect the natural world. Such events may also awaken us to blessings we often take for granted. And the beauty and the life-giving aspects of our natural world definitely call us to be good stewards of the planet on which we live.

I may have received my devotion to nature from my dad. Truly a man of the earth, my father loved to be outdoors. A landscaper by trade, he labored his whole life doing nursery work—planting trees and gardens, trimming shrubbery, and raising plants.

My mother has always been devoted to her faith. She attended church every week and taught Sunday school "religiously" for many years. My dad, on the other hand, preferred to do his worshipping in the outdoors. His faith, while he did not talk about it much, was expressed in the care he gave to his trees, shrubs, flowers, and the beauty of the natural world.

HE
THAT PLANTS A TREE
LOVES OTHERS
BESIDE HIMSELF.

THOMAS FULLER

My dad was a quiet man with a sly sense of humor, and his love of nature was second only to his love for his family. He kept bantam chickens as a hobby, and he loved feeding and watching birds in the backyard. When he retired from his landscaping job, he continued to raise small plants in his own nursery, often cultivating cuttings

FRANK CONSALEY
Small Nursery Stock

Shrubbery & Evergreens

from his own shrubs. He took real pride in the forsythia, arborvitae, hydrangea, azaleas, and boxwood plants he raised. Setting his plants out by our well-traveled road, he began selling them (practically giving them away) to passersby. A small business was born! Dad was so proud of his shrubs, and he took great pleasure when his customers returned to rave about how happy they were with his beautiful and thriving plants.

If that's not scattering joy, I don't know what is.

My love of flowers—a love that may be evident in my artwork!— is something I surely inherited from my dad. Although I enjoy cutting and bringing fresh bouquets indoors, my dad couldn't bear doing that. He saw this as shortening the lives of the flowers, and he much preferred seeing them in their natural setting. That difference of opinion caused a bit of friction for us. I can recall planting gladiola bulbs with him each year, and I couldn't wait to cut them into bouquets. I'd have to sneak them by my dad, though, in order to bring them into the house!

My father passed away in the spring of 2001—at the very peak of the most beautiful season of the year, when so many of his flowering plants were in bloom. Today, those plants continue to grow and bloom in the same beautiful and giving spirit with which they came into being.

Something to Think About:

Where is your favorite nature escape? What about that spot brings you joy?

I must

have

flowers

...always,

always.

Claude
Monet

Our
best teacher
is
our
own
heart.

Native American
proverb

TRUST YOUR GUT

Be who you are and say what you feel,
because those who mind
don't matter
and those who matter don't mind.

Dr. Seuss

When young artists ask me for advice, one thing I tell them is to be a sponge, to take in everything that goes on around them! I also encourage them to learn, observe, and study those they consider to be masters in their field. And then I tell them this: "Despite whatever you see and learn from artists around you, at the end of the day, be yourself."

Whether I've been in a professional or a personal situation, this advice has never failed me. After all, we can only become second-rate if we try to be an imitation of someone else. But if we are true to our own inner guidance, true to our own passions and talents, we can become the best possible version of ourselves. After all, it's our uniqueness that makes us truly special. Each of us has something to offer the world that no one else has. And while we can learn a vast amount from other people and though we can be influenced by current trends, it's our own interpretation of what we experience that makes our contribution valuable.

All of the talk about being oneself is much easier said than done. It takes a lot of courage to put yourself out there. After all, most of us are afraid that we aren't good enough, so we ask ourselves, *What if I fail?*

And let's not forget those times when we feel so lost in the muck of other people's expectations that we aren't quite sure who we are or what we have to offer. I think that of all the lessons I've learned—and that I keep re-learning—the most valuable one, and the hardest one for me to learn, unfortunately, is to trust my gut.

When something doesn't quite feel right to me or I'm torn over advice given to me by others, I sometimes make choices that aren't right for me. I keep learning the hard way that I'm best off when I act according to the voice inside of me.

One of these lessons in trusting my gut came while I was in college. I signed up for ceramics as an independent study course. The teacher was young and friendly, and I  felt I had established a good rapport with him in other classes I'd taken from him. Still, since an independent study course means no course outline, I was responsible for developing a plan and scheduling what I wanted to accomplish during the semester. I delayed doing anything, procrastinating and letting myself get caught up in various extracurricular pursuits. But I figured I could whip out some good work for this course rather quickly. I wasn't worried. After all, I had done well in previous courses with the same professor. I took for granted that I wouldn't have to sweat the grade in this class.

 Well, I really painted myself into a corner with my procrastination. I suddenly realized I only had a few weeks left to complete a semester's worth of work! Yikes! I didn't even have time to think clearly, much less carefully plan some interesting work. So, in my panic, I checked out every book in the college library on ceramics and pottery and started looking for ideas. This approach would have been fine if I'd started early enough to integrate that inspiration into my own work. But, running out of time, I feverishly completed what I felt were some pretty darn impressive

pieces based on what I saw in those books. I tried to put my own little spin on each piece as I completed it, but I'm sure that, as a collection, it was less than coherent. But I wasn't seeing it. I was just so relieved to have kept myself from falling flat on my face in my teacher's eyes.

Wrong again.

As kind as he was, my teacher was even wiser than he was kind. He knew enough about my earlier work to know that what I had produced in this independent study was not really me.

He gave me an F. *An F!!!* I was completely stunned. I thought I had an impressive array of pots—and I had delivered everything on time! The professor told me that he expected more of me and that he didn't see *me* in that work. Thankfully, he allowed me to take the course again. The second time around I produced some very imperfect plates and cups and sculptures and pots. But I put my heart into them, and he said it showed.

BE YOURSELF.
THERE IS NO ONE
BETTER QUALIFIED.

-ANONYMOUS

I discovered an important lesson about myself and about life from that experience in the ceramics studio. And I am grateful that my teacher had the courage to give me that F. He helped me learn yet again that I failed by not being true to myself and by not exercising my talents to the best of my ability.

Today I still struggle to trust my gut in both my art and my life. But I've learned that when I do, I am giving my best, my authentic self...and it always seems to show, no matter whom I might try to fool.

Something to Think About:

What decisions are weighing on you now? What does your gut tell you is the right path to choose?

JOHNNY BARNES

Those who bring sunshine to the lives of others cannot keep it from themselves.

James Barrie

SCATTER JOY SPOTLIGHT

Throughout this book, you'll find brief profiles of some very special people. So generous and thoughtful are their actions that we're shining the Scatter Joy Spotlight on them. You'll find another Spotlight profile wherever you see the Scatter Joy Spotlight symbol.

Every day of the week, retired bus driver Johnny Barnes rises before the sun and takes his place on one of Bermuda's busiest thoroughfares—and he has done so for more than a quarter of a century. From around 4 a.m. until 10 a.m., Johnny stands proudly and prominently at the curve of the Crow Lane Roundabout and does his self-assigned job.

Quite simply, Johnny has taken on the role of the island's goodwill ambassador, and he greets motorists, cyclists, and pedestrians on their morning commutes. He brightens everyone's day with a smile, a wave, and an occasional "Good morning!" or "God bless you!"[6]—and he asks nothing in return. Passersby can't help but respond with a friendly beep or a wave and almost always a smile. It's your guess as well as mine how many frowns he has turned into smiles with his simple, heartfelt gestures. Today, at age eighty-five, Johnny continues to scatter joy on Crow Lane every Monday through Friday.

By the way, Johnny has been married to his wife for fifty-seven years. According to him, she has a cheery disposition because he has "covered her with honey"[7] since they married in 1949.

To us,
family means

putting your arms
around each other
and
being there.

Barbara Bush

THE JOY OF FAMILY

Call it a clan, call it a network, call it a tribe, call it a family. Whatever you call it, whoever you are, you need one.

Jane Howard

Apart from those terrible adolescent years when we are desperate to separate from our family, most of us are blessed to know the love, comfort, warmth, and support of our families. Those who are not a part of a loving family often find one in a tight circle of friends who provide the unconditional love we all need to take for granted.

This whole "take for granted" issue is an interesting one. Of course it's important to express our love and gratitude to those people closest to us, but we *do* often take these loved ones for granted. And as long as we express our gratitude from time to time and return the love we receive, I say it's a good thing to be able to take something for granted in these uncertain times.

Isn't it gratifying to be able to count on the fact that each and every day the sun is going to rise in the morning and then set in the evening? We count on that; we pace our lives to this pattern. And thank goodness the sun's rhythm doesn't vary or we'd never get any sleep!

Similarly, we find peace of mind when we are able to count on certain events and specific people in our lives. Our faith is definitely one of the few, but critical sources of strength that we can count on. Next to our faith, our families can be a rock for us… as well as a source of pure joy!

Of course it's easy to find joy in our family when things are rosy. We celebrate birthdays and holidays, go on vacations, and enjoy day-to-day pleasures like family dinners (something that is a rarity in our too-busy world).

But when times are tough, we may argue, disagree, nag, or go without speaking to those we love. As hard as these spells are, we count on the fact that "this too shall pass," taking for granted— in a positive way—that the love in our family is unconditional love. We don't have to prove our worthiness or try to earn this love, but when we feel love's power, our natural tendency is to return that love.

For our family, one tradition that lasted many, many years was "Saturday Lunch." (Yes, we even called it by name.) Saturday, around noon, seemed to be the one time in our busy weekend that all of us were able to gather at my parents' house. Some weeks we had as many as nine or ten strong, and other times it might be only four of us. But, no matter what, come rain, shine, snow, sleet, or hail, we made our mecca to Mom and Dad's. Talk about taking something for granted! Saturday Lunch was a certainty like the rising of the sun, something that we could set our clocks to!

The Saturday Lunch meal featured pretty simple stuff, but two things were certain—there'd be iced tea and potato chips. (What more do you need anyway?) Sandwiches, pizza, and casseroles all rotated on the menu, but the warmth of the company, the camaraderie, the sharing of stories, the telling of jokes, and the rehashing of the week's news were the real reasons we attended. No matter what was happening in the world or in our lives, our simple Saturday Lunches were our port in the storm of our uncertain world.

LUNCHEON

When my daughter, Katie, was in her early adolescent phase of escaping behind the closed door to the private world of her bedroom, she was going through her growing pains—and taking us along for the ride! She didn't want to be seen with her family, and her friends became her whole world. She shared as little information as possible about her private life, her thoughts, her dreams, and her fears. It was a bit of an uncertain time for all of us, and we worried about whether she was growing up too fast or running with a too-wild crowd.

One Friday night she and her friends went to a dance club for underage kids. She was dressed to the hilt, full of herself and ready to experience this "clubbing" she'd heard so much about. She returned home by curfew and, no surprise, retreated into her private bedroom world. Minutes later, however, she emerged in tears and told me she didn't want to go to that place again! Apparently this walk on the wild side had come a little prematurely for her, and the crowd she thought was so cool now gave her a different vibe. From what she said, the place was very crowded and very loud. When it was time to leave, she couldn't find her coat anywhere.

Whatever happened that night was apparently a caution sign for her. (How gratifying for a mother to hear!) Katie was shaken up enough to let her mother see her tears and her fears, and that wasn't happening much during those years. We had a nice little talk, and after a good-night hug, she once again slipped behind her bedroom door into her private world. As I turned to walk away, though, I heard her open her door a crack and, in her small voice, say, "Mom, are you going to Saturday Lunch at Grandma's tomorrow?" When I said, "Of course!" she answered, "Me too." After all, it was our family's port in the storm.

Something to Think About:

What is your family's most treasured ritual? How often and how regularly do you practice that ritual?

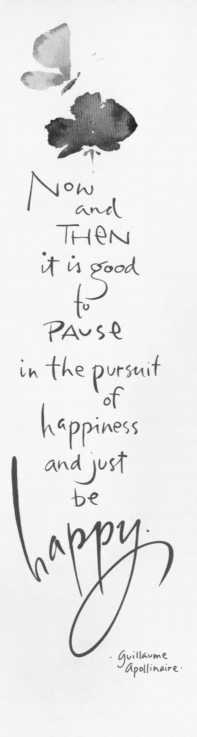

Now
and
THEN
it is good
to
PAUSE
in the pursuit
of
happiness
and just
be

happy.

. Guillaume
Apollinaire .

JOY SEEKER

Let a joy keep you.
Reach out your hands and take it
when it runs by.
Carl Sandburg

While attending a trade show in New York City several years ago, I was introduced to the creative director of a prominent book publishing company. Upon hearing my name, she replied, "I know you! You do such happy art. You must be such an upbeat person."

While her words were kind of nice to hear, they struck my funny bone. No one had ever described my work quite that way before, and I guess I never thought of myself as having a positive, happy outlook. When I told my husband, he got such a kick out of it that her comment has become a joke between us. "If only the world knew the *real* Kathy Davis!" he jokes. "And try living with her!"

Keep your
Sunny side up

Now, don't go thinking I am some mean or depressed ogre, but I certainly have my days. Like a good segment of the population, I am prone to worry and anxiety, with a dose of depression thrown in from time to time.

In fact, worrying seems to be a common malady in my overly sensitive family. Although I try hard to take preventive measures, heavy feelings often weigh me down. I'm particularly sensitive to the winter blues, and seasonal affective disorder (SAD) gets its grip on me, especially if I don't get a healthy helping of daylight. And when I'm in its grip, I tend to pull inside myself and snack too much (crunchy, salty, cheese crackers become my best friends). When I am trapped in the doldrums like that, I just want to pull the covers over my head and hibernate.

So, in thinking about the art and words that I feel driven to create, I am, in part, filling the need I have to avoid the blues; I am choosing to be a Joy Seeker. Building a reserve of energy with bright

colors and inspiring messages feeds my hunger for happiness. These messages speak to me and through me because I am searching for meaning in my own life and, while I'm at it, trying to make some positive difference, however small, in the world.

I do all of this because it feeds me. It makes me feel good, and I, for one, need a good amount of inspiration to function well from day to day.

In fact, for me, the creative process is often one big treasure hunt. I love to take in and absorb the colors, words, sights, sounds, patterns, and scenery all around me. Quotations, pages out of catalogs, eye-catching junk mail, photos, natural objects—you name it—I collect it. I am a certified pack rat! After this gathering phase of my creative process is over, I become a choreographer with the bits and pieces of inspiration I've collected, arranging them into something new based on my point of view. This is indeed a joyful process for me!

I guess you might call me a joy-aholic. I seek joy through my art. I seek joy through words and in experiences. I seek joy through simple pleasures, and I relish each and every one of them. I seek joy in my interactions with family, friends, and other people I meet. But, by far, the greatest satisfaction comes when I remember to share my joys with others. Even though I was never good at math, I do understand that joys multiply when they are divided!

Something to Think About:

Think about people you know. Who seems to live a joy-filled life? What do you think is the source or reason for that person's joy?

I'd like to share some of my favorite "joy" quotes.

May they inspire you as much as they do me!

Mark your days in ways that bring your heart joy.
Unknown

•

One must put all the happiness one can into each moment.
Edith Wharton

•

Joy seems to me a step beyond happiness.
Adela Rogers St. John

•

A merry heart maketh a cheerful countenance.
Proverbs 15:13

•

The time to be happy is now. The place to be happy is here. The way to be happy is to make others so.
Robert Ingersoll

•

Happiness is the result of making a bouquet of those flowers within reach.
Proverb

•

The best and most beautiful things cannot be seen or touched. They must be felt with the heart.
Helen Keller

•

When happiness gets into your system, it is bound to break out on your face.
Unknown

•

Awake at dawn with a winged heart and give thanks for another day of loving.
Kahlil Gibran

•

Happiness is as a butterfly which, when pursued, is just out of reach, but which if you will sit down quietly may alight on you.

Nathaniel Hawthorne

A Cherokee elder
spoke to his grandson,

"There are
two wolves

that live in our minds.

One is called Joy,
and he is filled with

happiness, peace,
harmony, and hope.

The other wolf is called Sorrow,
and he is filled with

negativity, jealousy,
anger, and guilt.

The two wolves
are always at battle."

The grandson asked his grandfather,

"Which wolf wins?"
. . . .

The grandfather answered,

"The one
you feed."

Native American wisdom

You
CANNOT BE
ANYTHING
IF YOU WANT
TO BE
EVERYTHING.

SOLOMON SCHECHTER

SELECTIVE MEDIOCRITY

Life does not have to be perfect to be wonderful.

Annette
Funicello

The human condition has never been easy. From the early quest for food and struggle to survive, to life before antibiotics and modern medicine, to the war and unrest of our day, challenges always plague us. So we simply can't wait for problem-free periods to experience joy... or we would be waiting forever.

While we have many advantages and conveniences in today's world, we too often suffer from symptoms of TMI (too much information). The fast pace of modern life can be overwhelming.

THIS MORNING
I WOKE UP TO A COLD, MISERABLE, RAINY DAY.
SO I PRAYED FOR THE STRENGTH
TO GET DRESSED AND RUN FIVE MILES.
THEN I ROLLED OVER AND WENT BACK TO SLEEP.
I HAD PRAYED FOR STRENGTH
BUT RECEIVED
WISDOM
INSTEAD.   ANONYMOUS

Add to that the pressure to be all knowing, to keep up with the latest technological advances, and to have that "perfect life." Well, guess what? That perfect life just ain't possible, dear reader. But you already knew that, didn't you?

Women in particular precariously juggle multiple roles and try hard to be all things to all people. Society's changes have been a catch-22 for women. The superwoman syndrome has trapped us all, and we don't appreciate it one bit. I'm not saying that we've given up. We all try our best to be attractive, educated, fun, nurturing, and successful. We strive to be perfect wives, wise mothers, loving daughters, devoted lovers, good girlfriends, and exemplary employees. And it's absolutely exhausting.

Way back when I was attending graduate school, a very wise woman professor of mine pulled me aside after an evening class of art education philosophy. Dr. B asked me to meet her in her office the following day. I wondered what was on her mind.

That next day, after some light conversation about class content, she gently broached a more personal topic with me. I was newly married and had been teaching for six years; I was earning two degrees during this year's leave of absence. Every day I was driving ninety minutes each way to college and back home again, working to excel at my studies, and trying to be that "perfect wife."

DON'T WORRY,
SPIDERS,
I KEEP HOUSE
CASUALLY.
KOBAYASHI ISSA

Dr. B explained that many years prior she had adopted a philosophy that she wanted to share with me. *Selective mediocrity* is the name she gave it—and I liked it already! She went on to explain that, while excellence is certainly an admirable goal, if we try to be excellent in each and every aspect of life, something will surely suffer.

Encouraging me to think hard about the things that truly mattered most to me, she recommended that I apply the standard of excellence only to my most important priorities. While there are oodles of requirements heaped on all of us, we don't need to hold ourselves to a standard of excellence for every single one of them. Dr. B suggested instead that we hold ourselves to a lesser standard when it comes to those demands that are not the top priorities in our lives.

I quickly embraced this philosophy and have become more than comfortable with being mediocre in certain areas of my life, areas that I am not passionate about. The principle of selective mediocrity has allowed me to

find more joy and meaning in those relationships and activities I really care about. Since adopting this liberating philosophy, I have also discovered that the world does, in fact, keep spinning even if some things aren't perfect. What a relief!

I am Woman.
I am Invincible.
I am Tired.

Something to Think About:
What do you tend to overdo that, if you didn't do it at all, might free you up for more important things?

•   •   •   •   •   •

Dr. B shared some of her tips with me. Here are just a few:

- Instead of worrying about having a perfectly clean house, just always make sure that your bathrooms are clean in case a guest drops by unexpectedly. Better yet, if economic circumstances allow, think about occasionally hiring cleaning help.

- Instead of trying to turn out a gourmet meal, take shortcuts. One of Dr. B's favorites was to pop a loaf of frozen bread in the oven. The smell is wonderful—and it suggests that you've slaved for hours.

- If you have children, don't be afraid to ask for help with them. Take turns sharing kids with a neighbor or family member in order to make some precious time for yourself. Then when you are with your kids, you can give them your total attention.

- Set boundaries for yourself even with the activities and responsibilities you are passionate about. You can't work seven days a week without eventually running out of steam.

PEOPLE IN OUR MIDST

Let us be grateful
to people who make us happy,
they are the charming gardeners
who make our souls blossom.

Marcel Proust

If you were having a dinner party and could invite six people from any point in history, whom would you invite? Every time I think about that question, I come up with different answers.

And that question prompts me to confess that watching the television series *Biography* is one of my addictions. People's life stories are full of interesting twists and turns.

The winding paths and experiences of our fellow travelers on Planet Earth are rich in their variety and complexity. The daily choices that we make guide and define our individual journeys. No two journeys—just like no two human beings— are ever quite the same. It's therefore no surprise that people provide an endless source of inspiration for me, in my work as well as in my life. Whether I know them personally or have simply read about them, people offer amazing examples of strength, kindness, and the resiliency of the human spirit.

So sometimes when I am struggling in my own life, I wonder, *What would so-and-so do?* I keep a mental list of the people I admire—mentors, teachers, even people I've only read about and heard about—who seem to really have their act together, who live in such a positive way. I think of these people as touchstones and find their examples helpful when I am seeking answers or guidance in my own life. When cluttered or conflicting thoughts trip me up or keep me stuck (as they often seem to do), I am able see the situation more clearly when I try to look at it through the eyes of one wiser than I.

Two of the people on my list of most inspiring examples are a couple we have come to know. Tom and Pat are among the friendliest, most well read, best educated, and wonderfully involved people on the planet. Quakers by faith, they walk their talk and live according to their values. They regularly attend Sunday meeting, and Pat often participates in peace marches. Both actively support the many causes they believe in, and both are politically active (although one is a Democrat and the other a Republican, a fact that sparks some lively debates!) As serious and committed as they are to their causes, Tom and Pat are just a hoot to be around! They have a true zest for life—attending symphony concerts and plays in the city (some twenty miles away), and never missing the fireworks at Penn's Landing at midnight every New Year's Eve. Their days are filled with gardening, reading, attending town meetings, traveling, and spending time with family and friends, yet they still manage to stay up to watch David Letterman every night. My husband Peter and I truthfully have a hard time keeping up with these two. Oh, and did I mention that Tom is ninety-three years old and Pat is just six years his junior? We've decided that we want to be like them when we grow up.

We first met these dear neighbors shortly after we moved into our new neighborhood about ten years ago. Peter was walking our 120-pound Newfoundland, Phoebe, in the woods when he heard another hiker on the trail exclaim, "What a marvelous animal!"

Enter Thomas, who was on an outing with his grandsons. Decked out in a bow tie and sports coat (which we've since learned is his everyday attire—even when he gardens!) and aided by a walking stick, Tom introduced himself as our neighbor on the other side of the woods. After effusively admiring Phoebe, Tom promised in his good neighborly way that he and Pat would invite us over for a visit someday soon.

The following weekend, after returning from some errands, we discovered a calling card in our front door. The card was inscribed with Thomas's full name and "Grindleton," the name of their centuries-old home. A handwritten line on the back of the card announced, "Come for tea! 4 p.m. Sunday." We had never received such an invitation. I asked Peter, "What do you suppose one wears to tea?"

Of course we accepted the gracious invitation, and we had a delightful time! We learned that Tom was a former teacher and Pat had been a realtor. They shared their personal stories about the rich history of our area, their family, their causes, their travels, their cottage in Maine, and their annual cricket match! Also, we learned that our town was named in honor of one of Tom's ancestors.

Tom and Pat have become dear friends, and we are constantly inspired and amazed by their

> THE PLEASANTEST THINGS
> IN THE WORLD
> ARE PLEASANT THOUGHTS,
> AND THE GREAT ART OF LIFE
> IS TO HAVE AS MANY OF THEM
> AS POSSIBLE.
> MONTAIGNE

wisdom, their down-to-earth attitudes, their outspoken opinions, their kindness, and their generous natures. They seize the gift of each and every day, and they find joy that others often miss. Tom does, however, admit to us, "Some days the news in the world really gets me down. It's then that I remind myself of the following passage":

> Whatsoever things are true, whatsoever things are honest, whatsoever things are just, whatsoever things are pure, whatsoever things are lovely, whatsoever things are of good report; if there be any virtue, and if there be any praise, think on these things. Philippians 4:8

•

These days, when I feel overwhelmed or find myself pulled down by negative thoughts, I reflect on that same verse from Philippians—and I am grateful for having been inspired by our dear friends on the other side of the woods.

Something to Think About:

What important lesson or truth have you learned from someone else?
What difference has learning that made in your life?

The time You
enjoy
Wasting
is
not
Wasted
Time.

Bertrand Russell

MAKING TIME FOR REJUVENATION

*Nowhere can man find a quieter
or more untroubled retreat
than in his own soul.*

Marcus Aurelius

I am absolutely convinced that time is our most precious commodity. And time for yourself must be of your *own* making. No one's going to hand it to you. The fact that we have so little time to begin with and that we require so much darn sleep (but I *do* savor my sleep) makes time very precious. Throw in all the demands on our time—our loved ones, our kids, our friends, our jobs, our communities, our causes. When the hours of the day get all divvied up, there is little or no time for ourselves. And, let's face it, we *all* need rejuvenation from time to time. Our batteries wind down and need recharging.

You are doing no one a favor by not taking a vacation—especially not yourself! Even taking just a five- or ten-minute break when you need one can work wonders for your sense of well-being.

But have you noticed that everyone seems to need something different to recharge? My husband prefers stimulating activity, meeting new people, learning new things. I, on the other hand, recharge most often by getting a change of scenery and going inside myself. My ideal getaway spot is the beach. The common thread of all recharging, though, may be a change of routine. And this can be as simple as going for a walk or as extravagant as taking a world cruise.

Communing with nature, going to museums, attending classes, traveling to new destinations, relaxing, being on a sports team, reading, writing, splurging on a night out or weekend away are all great ways to rejuvenate. In my experience, however, none of these is likely to happen without planning. You'll never just "find" free time. You have to make it—and then you have to take it.

When I know I have some beach time coming, I begin setting aside reading material—sometimes months in advance. I gather blank notebooks, stationery for writing letters, and articles I want to read.

Once I arrive, I find the beach almost instantly restorative. Something about the expanse of sea and sky helps me to breathe deeper. The tides are calming to me, and the enormity of the natural expanse makes me feel that I am a part of a world much bigger than myself. Being at the beach takes me outside of myself and my hectic daily world, while opening me up to new realizations about my life that I wouldn't otherwise uncover.

I return to my familiar surroundings somehow changed, somehow more me. The time away helps me to put things in proper perspective. Problems that previously seemed so important seem more manageable, and things I hadn't meant to be ignoring in my life may become new priorities for me.

Sure, in time that new perspective wears off, and I get whipped back into the frenzy of the everyday. But what I've gained doesn't ever fully go away.

So when I get stressed out, I remind myself that the beach is there waiting for me to discover new answers, insights, beauty, and, most of all, healing and renewal.

Something to Think About:

Think about to a time and place where you felt refreshed and rejuvenated. Where were you and what were you doing? When can you do this again?

MAISIE DEVORE

The only ones among you who will be really happy are those who will have sought and found how to serve.   Albert Schweitzer

Maisie DeVore, an eighty-three-year-old Kansas woman, is yet another Scatter Joy hero—in this case, heroine—with an inspiring story.

Maisie saw the need in her community for a public pool. She wanted the children in the area to have a place to swim. She wondered how she might take on that monumental project. So, more than thirty years ago, she started collecting tin cans, crushing them, and turning them into scrap metal for just five cents per pound. She selflessly toiled at her mission, month after month, driving her pickup truck in a forty-mile loop in search of cans. Amazingly, one can at a time, her efforts generated more than $73,000! Thanks to a matching grant, the funding needed to build the pool was now complete. Aptly named "Maisie's Community Pool" and located across the street from her home, the project was completed in 2001.

Maisie is one amazing lady! Her dream became a reality because of her "can-do" attitude! Today, she's still at it, collecting nine hundred pounds of cans each month (and now fetching thirty-four cents per pound) in order to help pay for the pool's maintenance.

One more note. Included in the pool's funding was a grant from actress Glenn Close, who starred in made-for-television movies based on the *Sarah, Plain and Tall* books. Maisie won a part in all three productions after answering the local newspaper's casting call for "weathered farm faces."[8]

a *kind*
word
is like
a spring day.
Russian proverb

KIND WORDS

*Kind words can be short
and easy to speak,
but their echoes are endless.*
Mother Teresa

Simple words can make a big difference. Scattering joy does not always involve a sacrifice or some monumental gesture of good will. A few thoughtful, sincere, and well-timed words can work wonders in a person's heart and cost us nothing when we share them with others.

There was a time when I envisioned myself in a career as a fine arts painter. After my kids were born, though, I barely found time for even the smallest of creative pursuits, let alone painting a 3'x 4' canvas.

So I gradually downsized my scale to a 5" x 7" size, which was perfect for greeting cards. But initially I felt that I had also downsized my career expectations when I acted on the realization that I might more easily earn a living with the smaller, more marketable format. I was stubborn at first, though, because I hated the idea that I was abandoning my fine art goals for a more commercial one.

Designing greeting cards pushed me into writing copy to accompany the art. I found that this came fairly easily to me, probably because I knew no rules at the time. I simply wrote the copy using the words I would say to someone.

Now, when I hear feedback from card buyers like, "You said exactly what I wanted to say, but I didn't know how," I feel so fortunate.

Not only do I get to be creative with my painting and designing, but I am also able to help others more clearly communicate to the people they care about. It doesn't get any better than that! Long ago I stopped regretting using my art and design as a commercial tool.

Kind words, encouraging words, appreciative words—they can do more than make our day; they can also have a lasting impression on us. And that statement is no surprise in this day when e-mail and texting seem to have taken over and, to some extent, replaced letter writing, face-to-face dialogue, and in-depth conversation. Words have even been replaced by acronyms, and *BFF, TBD*, and *LOL* have become our new shorthand. No wonder our spoken and written communications have become so precious.

As my career as a freelance artist grew into a small business, I found myself in the astonishing position of being a boss. But managing people, I found, was not all that different from being a teacher. Yet I had—and still have—a lot to learn.

One thing I have learned, though, is that—based on studies of employee satisfaction—the most important thing to an individual 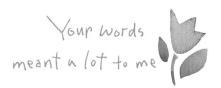 is recognition. That's even more important than financial rewards. Positive reinforcement for our efforts makes us feel valued. I know that, for me, nothing is as rewarding as receiving an e-mail from someone who has been touched by my work. Simple expressions of gratitude like that do a lot to keep me motivated. After all, every single one of us needs to feel that we are making some kind of difference in the lives of other people.

About ten years ago, I hired a really great guy whom I will call Sam. Although Sam had no solid experience for the job he was hired to do, he more than made up for it with his enthusiasm and willingness to do whatever needed to be done. Always giving his all, he asked for little in return. He was a true team player, and although I recognized that he always gave more than 100 percent, we were so busy and he was such low maintenance that he made it easy for me to take his efforts for granted.

> EVERYONE HAS AN INVISIBLE SIGN HANGING FROM HIS NECK, SAYING,
>
> "MAKE ME FEEL IMPORTANT!"
>
> MARY KAY ASHE

One day, when I noticed that he *again* surpassed expectations, without much thought, I grabbed a small Post-it note, scrawled, "*Great* job, Sam," and left it on his computer screen. Many months later, another member of our staff needed a ride home from work one day, and of course Sam obliged. He would always go out of his way for anyone.

The next day at work, the employee Sam had driven home mentioned to me that a worn out, weathered slip of paper—my Post-it note—was taped to the dashboard of Sam's car. My casual, spur-of-the-moment compliment had obviously made a big impression on Sam. I felt a little sheepish about my humble effort to encourage and appreciate him—and I realized that my employee recognition program could probably use an upgrade! However, I'm glad that my few simple words made such a difference to Sam. Clearly, communication—especially the communication of praise and affirmation—is powerful indeed.

One year, after my life eventually settled into a more serene place following my divorce, I felt some true healing taking place. Things started making sense and coming together for me. I guess you could say I got a new perspective. I decided to write a letter to my parents. Mind you, I saw my parents frequently since they lived nearby, but I knew I'd have an easier time expressing myself in writing rather than face to face.

While my divorce was devastating for my family, my parents came to accept it. In fact, they never wavered in their support for me and for my kids and even for my ex-husband. I felt such gratitude for my upbringing and for my parents' presence in my life through good times as well as bad. So I wrote and then *mailed* them the letter. I had no idea how they would respond to it. Being reserved—as they always had been—they politely thanked me for my letter. We never openly discussed it in any detail, and that was that…

Until many years later after my father passed away and we had to move my mother into an assisted-living home. While cleaning out their possessions, I discovered that very letter. My father had carefully folded it and placed it in his keepsake drawer, right alongside his army medals, baby pictures of his children, and other valuables. Then I knew just how important my words in that letter had been to my parents.

Something to Think About:

When was the last time you complimented someone else? How did saying those words make you feel?

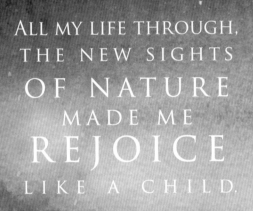

ALL MY LIFE THROUGH,
THE NEW SIGHTS
OF NATURE
MADE ME
REJOICE
LIKE A CHILD.

-MARIE CURIE

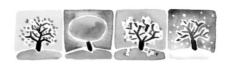

JOY THROUGH THE SEASONS

Live in each season as it passes:
breathe the air, drink the drink,
taste the fruit.

Henry David Thoreau

Our winters in the Northeast have been on the mild side in recent years, but still the season I most look forward to is spring. Sure, as a kid, I used to love ice skating and sledding and spending snow days off from school playing outdoors, untroubled by boots full of icy snow and fingers nearly frostbitten. But times have changed, and with each year I seem to have become more and more averse to winter. The loss of daylight seems to get to me the most. Cold air cuts through me like a knife, and I start shivering with the earliest autumn chill in the air. I am a true spring-summer spirit, and for half a year I would mourn the loss of my warm, light-filled days. Where's the joy in that?

So a few years ago when I came across Thoreau's call to "live in each season as it passes," those words hit home. Unless I was ready to move to a warmer climate, it was time for me to become a "coper" rather than a "moper." I decided to dig deeper and look for the joys that each season has to offer. This simple practice has helped me to appreciate the beauty and blessings that are around me throughout the year. Being mindful in each moment helps heighten our experiences. After all, time will steal those precious moments from us if we are not careful. Plus, I let myself find comfort in the predictability of the change in seasons. I discovered that tuning in fully to these cycles can work for me, not against me. The changing seasons provide variety and rhythm to life that I've learned to relish.

Here are some of the things that I enjoy about each of the four seasons.

SPRING — Springtime is at its most glorious when the tiny, bright green leaves burst forth and the flowering pear, crab apple, dogwood, and cherry trees create an explosion of pink and white blossoms. Wisteria, lilacs, and orange blossoms follow, perfuming the air with their fragrance. I love to walk in our nearby park, where the landscaping has been carefully orchestrated to allow each blooming row of trees to invite the next to follow its lead. Spring is a time of promise, hope, rebirth, and beauty.

SUMMER—There's nothing as magical to me as a summer evening. The longer days and warmer temperatures give us the gift of extended pleasures, allowing us to spend more time outdoors, taking in the aroma of freshly mowed grass, the sight of lightning bugs punctuating the twilight sky with their Tinkerbell magic, and the gleeful sounds of children's voices as they play outdoors into the evening hours. Summer's gift of longer days is surely one of my favorite things about this time of year.

FALL—I find the amber colors of autumn leaves truly amazing. I enjoy sweater weather, and I love hiking in the crisp air and watching migrating birds and butterflies, but I do feel a bittersweetness as nature's glorious show prepares for the next phase of life. I find myself slowly shifting indoors and making ready a cozy space for creative pursuits or curling up with a good book. Candles create just the right mood. With their warm glow and musky aromas, they soothe my spirit and provide the comfort I seek as daylight dwindles.

WINTER—Even though I do enjoy a stroll in the pure white beauty of a new snowfall, I'm pretty much prone to hibernate in the cold winter months. I prefer to be inside with a warm fire or wrapped up in the cocoon of a comforter. But one of my greatest joys during winter months has become feeding the birds and watching them flock to the feeding stations just outside of our windows. I spoil them with snacks of suet and sunflower seeds. The variety of offerings attracts chickadees, cardinals, finches, nuthatches, woodpeckers, and, oh yes, the ubiquitous squirrels too!

If you truly believe in scattering joy, why not try to do so all year long? As the writer of Ecclesiastes says, "To every thing there is a season" (v.3:1). Shouldn't we embrace and celebrate the joys in every season, too?

Something to Think About:

Which season of the year do you find the most challenging? What would help you enjoy this season more?

FINDING JOY AS WE TRY TO FIND BALANCE

Our greatest danger in life is in permitting the urgent things to crowd out the important.

Charles E. Hummel

One of the keys to a joyful life, I have found, is balance. And when it comes to determining how balanced my life is, a bird's-eye view of the big picture is more helpful than a focus on daily activities. Rarely do I have what I would call a well-balanced day. Hard as I try, most days are moved along by various demands, needs, and urgencies.

We all wear many hats in life. No matter who we are, most of us have multiple roles, juggling our friends, spouses, and parents with the needs of our children and our work lives. A perfect day would probably include time for us to indulge in each one of those ourselves. But that's pretty unrealistic, huh?

I do feel best when my life is in balance, when I'm attending to every need and doing justice to my different roles, but most often I find myself pretty immersed in one role or another. These days, my work tends to get more of my attention than other things, and even then it's often one particular aspect of my job that has my full attention.

Still, the challenge of keeping my plates spinning has always plagued me. After all, it seems obvious to me that to do something well, I need to completely focus on that task. So rather than doing justice to many things at the same time, I am actually just shifting my attention from one task to the next—and, at least in my experience, getting pretty lackluster results most of the time.

> IF THIS WERE
> A FANTASY WORLD,
>
> ~
>
> THERE WOULD BE
> TEN OF ME
> & WE WOULD
> EACH BE DOING
> WHAT WE
> WANTED TO DO.
>
> GEORGE LUCAS

As you attempt to achieve that elusive balance in life, be aware that the things itching for attention are too often what I call the small urgencies, like responding to e-mail and returning phone calls. Unless we are careful, our days can become consumed with these reactionary activities instead of the more *important* but often less urgent uses of our time.

Being a mom has helped me become more patient with myself and more accepting of my efforts to maintain a balanced life. Watching my kids grow up and move through various ages and stages of development has shown me that nothing ever stays the same. We may feel somewhat off balance or stuck in certain stages; or we may feel that we have little control over our time. I have learned that these seasons, too, will pass.

I have also learned where I need to go to relax, and for me, most often, that's the beach. As a child, I played in the waves; as a teenager, I walked with friends on the beach and boardwalk; and as a young adult, I relaxed in the sun with a good book. The beach has always been a place of escape and rejuvenation for me.

When I became a new parent, I looked forward to sharing my love for the shore with my family. That is, until reality hit. Setting up camp—complete with playpen, umbrella, sunscreen, and all the equipment necessary for caring for my young son for a day on the beach —was absolutely exhausting.I definitely wasn't used to it, and that was just the beginning! I soon realized that looking after my toddler—surrounded by sand begging

Little Ben on the beach

to be eaten, water luring his tiny footsteps, and seagulls swooping down for handouts—was a demanding and relentless job of policing! Not that I didn't find joy in watching my son splash in the waves and run down the beach after sandpipers, but I had to laugh at myself for packing my beach books and preparing to relax as I was used to doing!

My rejuvenation time on the beach turned into something completely different, something that, to be honest, was even more enjoyable, but I figured that the days when I could read and take a nap in the summer sun by the shore were gone forever. Now that my kids are grown, however, I have plenty of time for my reading and unwinding down by the sea. Ironically, I spend much of that time looking forward to visits from them when they can take time from their busy lives to join me. I still relish watching them enjoy themselves on the beach or in the surf with their friends. Sharing beach time with my family has become very precious to me.

Yes, I felt as though my life was a bit out of balance when my kids were younger and needing my constant attention, but now I realize that those times passed all too quickly.

So I guess what we need most when we're looking at our lives is perspective. Again, while my life doesn't necessarily feel particularly balanced on a day-to-day basis, when I consider the span of my life and the roles I've been privileged to play so far—that is, when I look at my life from a bird's-eye view—I'm surprised to find that it looks pretty darn balanced after all.

Something to Think About:

What in your life seems to constantly throw you off balance? What step(s) can you take toward living a more balanced life?

JACK MCSHANE

*How wonderful it is that nobody need wait
a single moment before starting to improve
the world.*   Anne Frank

Sometimes the problems in the world and even in our local community seem overwhelming, and we feel helpless in our ability to make any difference, let alone scatter joy. But the story of Jack McShane, a thirteen-year-old from New Orleans, reminds us that one person *can* make a difference.

In the aftermath of Hurricane Katrina, as the city struggled to rebuild and regain some of its former glory, many people understandably either gave up and relocated or gave in and accepted the broken spirit affecting much of the city. But not Jack.

Frustrated by the lack of attention given to New Orleans City Park, where he had played sports for years, Jack commented, "It just bothered me that it didn't look good."[9] So he decided to take positive action, and just about every Saturday morning, Jack can be found mowing one small part of the park's 1300 acres. Others have joined him in overcoming the destruction caused by Katrina, and the "Mow-Rons," his grass roots mowing club (www.mow-rons.org),[10] has become officially established as a nonprofit charity. Their original slogan—"The mow-rons are in City Park; the idiots are in City Hall"—has been changed to "Weeding by Example," because the first was, in Jack's words, "a little bit inappropriate."[11]

Jack's positive example is just one way that one person's actions can prompt an entire movement and make a huge difference in the lives of many people.

LETTING JOY OVERCOME GUILT

Love yourself - accept yourself - forgive yourself - and be good to yourself, because without you the rest of us are without a source of many wonderful things.

Leo F. Buscaglia

I know, for me, while I was blessed to grow up in a loving home with wonderful parents and a so-so brother (just kidding, Freddie boy), guilt was nevertheless alive and well. I felt guilt about spending money, wasting time, getting too silly, watching too much TV, sleeping too late, being too self-centered, or being vain—and all that's in addition to the guilt I felt about the big stuff, those things I did that I knew were not right.

But why do we so often feel guilty about taking care of ourselves? I'm not sure I have the answer to that question, but I am happy to say that I have made great strides in overcoming the guilt I used to experience when I was being good to myself and taking time for myself. Sadly, my parents' generation missed out on healthy doses of self-indulgence. For me, a massage, going for a walk, having *nondiet* ice cream on occasion (Häagen-Dazs coffee—there's nothing else like it!), or buying a new pair of shoes does wonders for the soul!

My parents, however, were lifelong subscribers to the Puritan work ethic. Don't get me wrong—this commitment to hard work is a good thing when it's not taken to extremes. But I remember them going outside in three feet of snow after a blizzard, each with a snow shovel in hand, to furiously dig their way out of our long driveway in order to get to work on time. Sure, I admired their dedication and determination, but at times it seemed to border on insanity.

Living through the Great Depression also made a huge impression on Mom and Dad, and of course much of this filtered down to Fred and me. We were taught not to waste anything—not time, money, clothes, or food. To this day, my mother (at age ninety!) will clean her plate each and every time even if it pains her—unless we notice her struggling to finish and clear the table! She could be a bit healthier and enjoy a good meal a bit more if she could get rid of her "Depression Era" mentality and stop thinking about the starving children in Africa long enough to consider her own health.

My mother has had a fulfilling and comfortable, if simple life, and she has definitely done more than her share of scattering joy. I just wish she could have learned that it's not just okay to be good to yourself, that it's more than okay. It's actually good for you!

Be good to Yourself

Shortly after my divorce when I was on my own with my two young kids, my mother stopped by to give me a hand as she (thankfully) often did. I had just returned from the grocery store and finished putting away the food when she came in through the back door to the kitchen. I was arranging the cut flowers I had just bought, placing them in a vase for the kitchen table. I could tell that she was troubled.

When I asked her what was wrong, she confronted me about the flowers, asking me if some new admirer had sent them (of which she would definitely have disapproved!). After all, the divorce was so very difficult for my parents to accept, and my dating so soon when I had two little kids depending on me would have been too much for my mother to handle. I thought I was off the hook when I replied, "No, I bought them for myself!" My mother looked absolutely stunned. Obviously she never bought herself flowers (how wasteful, frivolous, and self-indulgent!), and she couldn't quite fathom that I had done so for myself—especially when I should be "in mourning" over my divorce and focused on my children.

Now, I love and admire my mother very much, and I will never come close to her good works and almost sainthood status, but I've become quite comfortable being my own best friend and not feeling guilty about treating myself well.

These days I try to buy myself flowers every week. Doing so brings me such joy! And when I buy flowers for myself, I often pick up a bouquet for my mother to brighten her assisted-living apartment. I think she might just enjoy those flowers as much as I enjoy giving them!

Something to Think About:

What simple thing can you, acting as your own best friend, do for yourself?

Live
Laugh
Love

JOY THROUGH HUMOR

*God bless the good-natured,
for they bless everybody else.*

Henry Ward Beecher

You often hear that one of the most desirable traits a single person looks for in a potential mate is a good sense of humor. To that I say, "Bravo!"

As challenging as marriage can be, a shared sense of humor can help carry you through the tough times. At times, I find my husband to be a pretty frustrating and high-maintenance individual. (My guess is that you may be able to relate?) But, thank goodness, he can always make me laugh.

And, even better, I can make him laugh too. Honestly, the fact that he gets such a kick out of me is one of the things I find so attractive about him.

Who doesn't want to make people laugh? Now, I'm the lousiest joke teller in the world. I couldn't tell a joke if my life depended on it—I never even seem to remember them. But I do love a good laugh! For me, Ellen DeGeneres can always turn my blue mood into a rosier one. I TiVo® her show and, when I need it, watch a segment or two before I go to bed at night to relax and put my mind into a happy place. Sometimes I just watch the little dance she does to kick off her show. It never fails to make me smile!

> THAT DAY IS
> LOST
> ON WHICH
> ONE HAS NOT
> LAUGHED.
>
> FRENCH PROVERB

Thank goodness for Ellen and nutty people like her—because people like me really need them. I tend to be a pretty introspective person, and without realizing it, I can pull myself down and into a funk rather easily. I never really thought much about this until a free-spirited person I barely knew happily pointed this out to me.

I was in my thirties when I took a weeklong calligraphy workshop. Our final assignment was to hand-letter a quote of our choosing and decorate the page. Our class would then put together a small limited-edition book, and we'd each get a copy. As seems to be the

case in every gathering, the class had one real live wire—an outspoken woman who seemed to live life on a whim. I always look in awe at those souls who were somehow born with such joie de vivre!

Most of my classmates were more experienced calligraphers, and they seemed to have become friends after taking numerous courses together. I definitely felt a little out of my element. Being a novice at calligraphy and not knowing anyone in the class, I was fairly quiet. I chose to just sit back and absorb what I could. So when it came time for me to present my project to the group, I was feeling a little self-conscious. The quote I picked was a bit introspective, something like "It is every step of the journey that matters, not just the destination."[12]

YOU ARE ONLY GIVEN
A LITTLE SPARK OF
MADNESS.
YOU MUSTN'T LOSE IT.

ROBIN WILLIAMS

When she heard my quote, the gregarious woman blurted out, "Geez, some people need to lighten up!" I'm sure I blushed scarlet that day.

Well, I still love that quote, but what that woman said that day made a lasting impression on me. I *do* tend to take things too seriously, and I need to remind myself to keep a light heart. After all, there's no joy like the joy of laughter. A little levity can turn adversaries into compatriots. It can turn a tough day right on its head, heal like medicine, and even turn an argument into a meeting of the minds. We all love to feel good, and a dose of laughter is a tonic like no other.

(Oh, in case you're wondering, the woman's quote was "Life is short, so eat dessert first"!)[13]

ADDENDUM: A BAD CASE OF THE CHURCH GIGGLES

There is something particularly delicious about laughing when you aren't supposed to. The inappropriateness of laughing in church  during a sermon or a formal function can capture the best of us. This happened to me right in the middle of a parent-teacher conference—and I'm embarrassed to admit that I was one of the teachers!

As a five-teacher team, we met our students' parents together so that we could address all the coursework in the same meeting. I can't even recall what set it off, but one of the teachers was struck silly by something the parent said, and this obviously inappropriate response set off a chain reaction unlike anything I've ever witnessed. Trying to control this inappropriate laughter was impossible. Four of us became weak with insane giggling to the point of tears rolling down our cheeks. Thank goodness one of the

IF YOU TICKLE **YOURSELF**, YOU CAN LAUGH WHEN YOU LIKE.

RUSSIAN PROVERB

teachers was able to carry on for the rest of us blithering idiots.

Of course we later apologized to the understanding parent for our terrible behavior, but the very thought of that day still makes me feel giddy.

Something to Think About:

What funny situation, comment, or experience makes you smile every time you think about it?   What can you do to keep moments like these woven into your daily life?

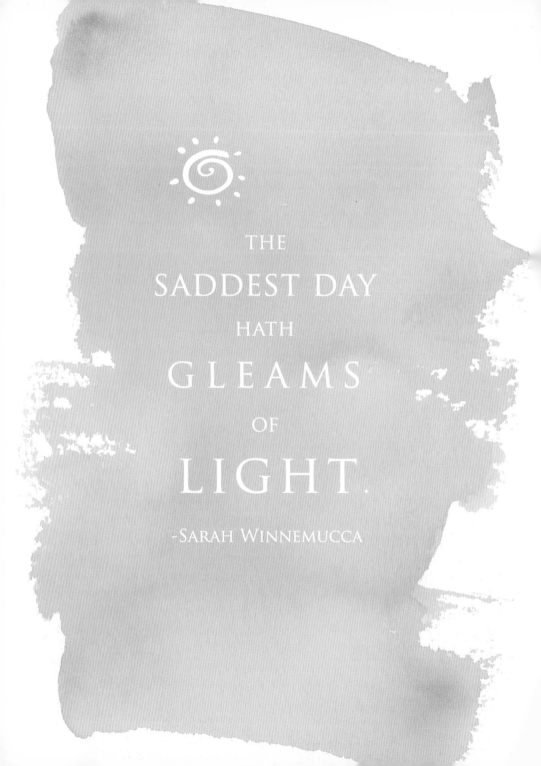

THE

SADDEST DAY

HATH

GLEAMS

OF

LIGHT.

-SARAH WINNEMUCCA

JOY IN ADVERSITY

We could never learn to be brave and patient if there were only joy in the world.
— Helen Keller

I remember a time when I was truly torn over a decision in my life's path. I talked it out, struggled with the pros and cons, examined it from every angle... and was still stymied. It was then that a friend who I had confided in sent me this quote by Rainer Maria Rilke: "Live your questions now, and perhaps even without knowing it, you will live along some distant day into your answers."

Sometimes answers are just not *ready* to be made.

Sometimes a problem doesn't have a clear-cut solution, and we need to find a way to cope.

one day at time.

Sometimes even our prayers don't bring answers as readily as we'd like.

A serious illness or the loss of a loved one greatly impacts our lives and leaves us numb with pain or loss. When my dad suffered a serious stroke and was incoherent for days before he started to improve, the pain that my family and I felt was truly oppressive. I remember waking each morning with the weight of the world clouding my consciousness; I did not want to face the day and deal with the pain that I knew was lying in wait....

OUR LIVES ARE LIKE THE COURSE OF THE SUN.

AT THE DARKEST MOMENT THERE IS THE PROMISE OF DAYLIGHT.

UNKNOWN

A month or so ago, when I was deep in worry about some problems of my own, I forced myself to take a walk. Feeling pretty low, I decided to go to the memorial park nearby to clear my head a bit. I love going there because it is so beautifully landscaped, and the small green buds were tight on the trees. Feeling so buried in my worries and my work, I was afraid I might miss spring if I weren't careful. Since the season was just on the verge of exploding, I thought I might feel better if I let nature help soothe my soul. Another reason I love going to the park is because my dad is buried there, and I always feel better being close to his memory.

After a brisk stroll along the pathways, I started to sense some much-needed perspective returning to me—and at that moment I came upon a group of people walking away from a funeral that had just concluded. I noticed that most of the people were young, and then I saw the uniforms. It dawned on me that another one of our young soldiers must have been lost in the war. I was overcome by the sadness and numbness that these young friends must have been experiencing in their loss.

My problems were still with me, but suddenly they didn't seem nearly as serious as they had just moments before. After all, I was not only going to have the chance to work through those problems, but I was also going to be around to watch those buds on the trees explode into bright green leaves...unlike the young soldier who lost his life.

Some days we have to drag ourselves through challenges that seem insurmountable and pain that borders on unbearable. In times like that, we need to ask for help from above or from a support system of friends and family. We can also benefit from the wisdom and perspective of others.

Here are some of the quotes and inspiring words that have helped me when times are toughest:

Weeping may endure for a night, but joy cometh in the morning.
Psalm 30:5

For a long time it seemed to me that real life was about to begin, but there was always some obstacle in the way. Something had to be got through first, some unfinished business... then life would begin. At last, it dawned on me that these obstacles were my life.
Bette Howland

Anyone can give up, it's the easiest thing in the world to do. But to hold it together when everyone else would understand if you fell apart, that's true strength.
Theodore Roosevelt

When nothing seems to help, I go look at a stone cutter hammering away at his rock perhaps a hundred times without as much as a crack showing in it. Yet at the hundred and first blow, it will split in two, and I know it was not that blow that did it, but all that had gone before.
Jacob Riis

Let me not pray to be sheltered from dangers, but to be fearless in facing them. Let me not beg for the stilling of my pain, but for the heart to conquer it.
Rabindranath Tagore

Love conquers all.
Virgil

I can be changed by what happens to me, but I refuse to be reduced by it.
Maya Angelou

The sun shines brighter after a shower.
Yiddish proverb

Notice that the stiffest tree is most easily cracked, while the bamboo or willow survives by bending with the wind.
Bruce Lee

So, you say, there is patience, there is acceptance, there is resilience, there is release… but what about *joy*?

As hard as life can sometimes be, I have learned that joy can and does exist despite pain. We must simply be open to it. Not only can we be surprised to experience these joyful moments, but they often take on a beauty and poignancy that they don't have when life is easy.

I liken this experience to times when I've tried to diet, times when I avoid food I crave, food that is loaded with unhealthy ingredients. Dieting and deprivation don't feel so good! At first, the simply prepared foods of my diet—as healthy as they are—seem bland

and uninteresting compared to Cheez Doodles® and cream-filled chocolate cupcakes. But soon, after accepting the changes to my diet, I find that even the smallest snack of grapes or an apple can taste absolutely delicious. Who'd have thought? My point is this: I come to appreciate the simple goodness I had overlooked before. Our senses can become dulled from overload. We become more sensitive to our surroundings when our perspective changes.

So it is with joy. When times are tough, we have a heightened awareness and appreciation of simple joys that we may have otherwise overlooked. A simple hug, reassurance from a friend, or a kind gesture from a loved one all become priceless to us.

Letting yourself feel joy in the midst of a sorrowful situation is often a matter of maintaining your perspective, appreciating small blessings, and keeping an open heart.

Something to Think About:

Who among your family, friends, and acquaintances is going through a tough time? What can you do to help?

THE GEM
CANNOT
BE POLISHED
WITHOUT
FRICTION,
NOR MAN
PERFECTED
WITHOUT
TRIALS.

CHINESE PROVERB

BILL SAMPLE

SCATTER JOY
SPOTLIGHT

*The surest path to happiness
is in losing yourself
in a cause greater than yourself.*
Unknown

Bill Sample is a former Philadelphia police officer. In the 1960s, Bill's beat included a children's hospital. Encountering many critically ill children, he was touched by the unfairness of their plight. Forging many friendships with those young children, Bill began asking them, "What would be your one special dream?"

Knowing that their families were burdened by medical bills, Bill took out a personal loan and, with the help of other generous and compassionate people, started to turn dreams into reality for those seriously ill children. And the Sunshine Foundation was born.

Today, the foundation continues to make dreams come true for children who are critically ill, physically challenged, or abused. Bill definitely started some serious joy scattering!

• • •

For more information about the Sunshine Foundation, visit

scatterjoy.com

or

www.sunshinefoundation.org.

*Do you know
someone who belongs
in the
Scatter Joy Spotlight?*

*Visit scatterjoy.com
and let us know!*

Beauty
can be
found in
unexpected places.

SCATTERING JOY WITH FAMILY

*If you light a lamp for somebody,
it will also brighten your path.*

Buddhist saying

A couple years ago, when my two children were entering young adulthood, we decided to spend our family vacation time in New Orleans and Mississippi. We wanted to help with Hurricane Katrina disaster relief. News of the destruction to the region permeated the media, and the needs seemed to be overwhelming. While it wasn't the kind of vacation we were used to, we all agreed that the trip was important. My husband, Peter, signed the four of us up with a group from our local church to work with the Presbyterian Disaster Relief organization.

Planning for our time away, we packed old clothes, tools, band-aids, and bug spray. We also mentally prepared ourselves for hot, muggy weather, sleeping in tents with mosquito nets, and rustic outhouse accommodations. At the same time, we educated ourselves about the devastation and learned about some of the experiences of the survivors. We were not skilled construction

from New Orleans to Biloxi . . .

workers by any means, but we hoped we would be able to help make a difference in some way. What we were *not* prepared for was the impact that trip would have on us....

Just as we'd been warned, the devastation was vast, the suffering was overwhelming, and the need was great. In our makeshift campsite in Mississippi, we got dressed each morning and packed our lunch. Then we were ready and willing to go wherever they needed us most. Fortunately, the four of us were often assigned to the same project, helping rebuild one of the thousands of decimated homes in the region. We honed our skills as we went along, as we sanded, drywalled, cleaned, and gutted houses that had been flooded with up to ten feet of water.

Our kids, Ben and Katie, were twenty-four and twenty-one at the time, and they had not had any prior experience with the kind of work we were doing. Actually, they were pretty used to the good life, usually tied to their cell phones and computers and focused on having fun with their friends. Peter and I weren't sure how they would handle the week.

mile after mile of devastation

As is pretty typical for young adults in their early twenties, Ben and Katie were in a place of uncertainty in their lives. They had spent their college years searching for a major that felt right for them. Lacking clear direction for their futures, neither of them seemed to feel overly confident about their skills or what they could contribute to the Katrina cleanup project. They looked forward to lending a hand in Mississippi, but they questioned just how they might be useful. Little did they know that they were about to show us a thing or two....

Usually quiet and reserved with strangers, Ben became a different person when he interacted with the workers and residents. Although he had no prior construction experience, he totally immersed himself in each task and learned many different skills from some of the experienced workers on the job. Ben gained some valuable training in doing drywall and carpentry, training that he never would have been exposed to elsewhere, and this new knowledge helped him develop some confidence in his ability to do things he never would have dreamed he could do. And seeing the way he was extending himself to strangers in need filled me with pride. What a fine young man Ben had become! I saw a mature side of him that I wasn't able to see at home.

Ben immersed in his work

And then there was Katie, who took to her new role with gusto. Usually laid back, carefree, and a bit lazy at home, she kicked in like a dynamo. I watched with amazement when she volunteered for extra kitchen duty and when she was appointed foreperson on one of the jobs I was assigned to. Was this tough and demanding boss really my kid? On this trip, I also realized that Katie craves structure and loves being busy—character traits I had never noticed on the

Katie making friends at our campsite

home front. Having found the volunteer work very rewarding, she has returned to Mississippi a second time, taking a friend along to help. She is now considering other types of outreach work in her future.

Seeing my grown children involved in the Katrina project gave them (and me) a new perspective on life and on their place in the world. I saw Ben and Katie in a new light while they were busily focused on helping others. I liked what I saw in them, and I realized that they will find their way in the world and do just fine.

•   ◦   •

The four of us took some time to drive along the coastline from Biloxi, Mississippi, to New Orleans, and we witnessed mile after mile of destruction. Families without homes were temporarily living in FEMA trailers, dependent on others to help them put their lives back together. Their spirits, however, were strong and determined. Worse than this loss of homes, though, was the irreplaceable loss of loved ones that others suffered.

IT IS ONE OF THE MOST **BEAUTIFUL** COMPENSATIONS OF THIS LIFE

•   •   •

THAT NO MAN CAN SINCERELY **TRY TO HELP ANOTHER** WITHOUT **HELPING HIMSELF.**

RALPH WALDO EMERSON

As we drove along the coastline that day, the four of us said very little to one another. Words just weren't necessary. The situation we witnessed together made us stronger as individuals and as a family. And the gratitude we felt for our lives, our blessings, and the love we shared was very clear. Furthermore, having

worked together in a way we never had before and in a situation that humbled us, we came away with a new appreciation for one another. We may have been able to make some small difference to one town in Mississippi, and what we gained as a family were the blessings we received in return.

We definitely got back more than we gave that spring of 2006.

Something to Think About:

What activity can you do with your family or friends to help make a difference in the lives of people less fortunate than you?

GOING WITH THE FLOW

Go as the way opens.
Quaker proverb

Where would we be without goals? They give us a sense of purpose, something valuable to strive for, and they help guide our steps toward that end. But I have also discovered that staying open to change is just as valuable as setting and working toward goals.

If we pursue goals blindly and relentlessly, we risk missing out on opportunities that present themselves along the way. It takes courage to stay open to the unexpected and to take detours we weren't planning for, but the rewards are often well worth it.

Many years ago, with a new son in our lives, my former husband and I decided to become members of my mother's church. Our pastor was young, and he had a friendly, contemporary approach that prompted some of the old-timers to scratch their heads. To become new members, we were required to attend weekly sessions with other prospective members. We got to know one another as we learned more about the church and its teachings.

During one of these sessions, the pastor asked us to consider certain questions. One question that I still remember was "What would you rather be—a sailboat or a motorboat?" I loved that question and the thoughts it prompted. I immediately answered, "Sailboat" because I'd much rather glide with the direction of the wind, making little noise and causing little disruption. The freedom, beauty, and effortless movement of a sailboat appeals to me much more than a loud motorboat speeding across the water.

I still think about the analogy. At certain times I have needed to fight against the current and make noise in order to get someone's attention. But what usually works better for me, what tends to feel more comfortable, is waiting for the right winds. Of course I need to be prepared and in the right place when the winds come my way. But I'd rather invest energy in that kind of preparation than in pushing against the current. That can really wear me down.

I have become very sensitive to which activities give me energy and which sap my energy. In fact, I keep a list of "Energy Givers" and "Energy Drainers" as I notice them affecting my outlook. I've tried to find ways to minimize those draining activities or delegate them to people who actually get energy from what drains me.

My mother always said that she'd rather make money doing something she liked and then pay someone to do the things she didn't like, and the apple didn't fall very far from the tree! I find her comment funny, though, when I think about it now, because there's very little my mother didn't do herself. In that way, she and I are very different!

When life situations get tough and challenges seem insurmountable, I often struggle, looking for answers. During these times, when I can, I escape to the beach where I either seem to discover an answer, get a better perspective on the circumstances, or simply realize just how minor my problems are in the scope of things.

> IT IS A GREAT PIECE OF SKILL
> TO KNOW
> HOW TO GUIDE YOUR LUCK
> EVEN WHILE WAITING FOR IT.
>
> BALTASAR GRACIAN

Just last year, my company was going through a dramatic transition, and I faced some serious decisions. Of course I headed to the beach, which was especially peaceful and calm because it was the off-season. I walked for miles, seeing almost no one and enjoying being lost in my thoughts. It was then I noticed them—a school of dolphins swimming very close to shore. I'd never seen dolphins up so close, and I felt drawn to them as I watched them joyfully glide through the waters. Migrating dolphins can travel great distances, yet their journey appears so easy and elegant as they go with the flow.

That's when it struck me: I needed to go with the flow, too. My journey didn't need to feel so burdened. I could choose the option that felt natural to me. So, even when solutions to problems aren't clear, I can live my life with less stress and effort as I wait for insight and guidance.

The sight of the dolphins lifted my spirits that day. When I returned to my beach chair, I grabbed my journal and wrote inside the cover: "When life gets tough…remember the dolphins!"

Something to Think About:

What activities and relationships give you energy? What activities and relationships take away your energy? What can you do to reduce the energy drainers in your life?

All the flowers
of
tomorrow
are in the seeds
of today.

anonymous

JOY WORTH WAITING FOR

Faith is the substance of things hoped for, the evidence of things not seen.

Hebrews 11:1

As I sit down to my writing on this snowy February day, I have visions of May and the flowers that will bloom their heads off as they do year after year. So this weekend I will shop for some seeds, soil, and growing pots in anticipation of spring. We recently refurbished a small greenhouse that adjoins our home. It had been sitting empty and unused for the past dozen or so years. (Well, it wasn't exactly empty. It had accumulated plenty of stuff, as unused spaces tend to do.)

When we were looking for a home to buy back in the early nineties, this greenhouse was one of the things that first attracted me to our property. But the years since have been consumed by much busyness—by growing children, aging parents, and the demands of building businesses while keeping all our other plates spinning. The greenhouse quickly fell to the bottom of our "to do" list.

Until this past year. I found myself with a newly emptied nest and a growing desire to see green growth even during the dead of our northeast winters, so the greenhouse started to climb in priority.

Just as my enthusiasm began reaching a fever pitch, though, we discovered that the oil burner that keeps the greenhouse going through the cold months was completely kaput. With a new heater priced beyond reach (as were oil prices!), I quickly tabled the greenhouse project in order to avoid the cost of winter heating. I was disappointed, but I made peace with the setback. That is, until my thoughtful husband surprised me with a shiny new blue oil burner for Christmas! (Now how many women can boast about that?) He also included a gift certificate for some plants. Yes! Green in the dead of winter! And so, on this snowy February day, my greenhouse is almost as green as I had imagined—and I'm eager to try my first seed-sprouting experiment! I know I'll need to wait patiently for my seeds to grow into flowers, but I have faith that the flowers will indeed bloom one day in May.

Faith. We put it into action when we invest in and pursue our dreams, and that process requires faith, patience, and perseverance. Just like the slowly sprouting seeds in a greenhouse, my dream of having a business of my own was built slowly—one small greeting card at a time. My dream-turned-reality took many years and lots of hard work, patience, resilience, and, above all, faith!

all things grow with love.

Something to Think About:

What positive action can you take today that may sow seeds for rewards and joy in the future?

OSEOLA MCCARTY

*Give what you have. To someone, it may
be better than you dare to think.*
Henry Wadsworth Longfellow

Oseola McCarty was truly a woman of faith.

This simple Mississippi woman supported herself by doing laundry until she retired...at age eighty-six. As a child, Oseola had hoped to become a nurse, but she had to leave school when she was in the sixth grade to help her family with finances. She became a laundress, washing and ironing other people's clothes just as her grandmother, mother, and aunt had done before her. For over seventy years she toiled, saving just a dollar or two at a time. Taking pride in her work, she lived simply, trusted God to care for her, and saved her money. Then, when she retired in 1994, she quietly donated $150,000—which was most of her life's savings—to start a college scholarship fund at the University of Southern Mississippi. This fund would provide for needy students and enable them to have the education she never did.

This amazing gesture from the then eighty-eight-year-old woman—who appeared to have so little—had an impact far beyond her expectations. You see, once word of her generosity spread, Oseola's charity inspired countless others—including business, political, and community leaders—to match her giving spirit. For instance, upon hearing of Oseola's gift, multibillionaire Ted Turner donated a billion dollars to charity, saying, "If that little woman can give away everything she has, then I can give a billion."[14] McCarty's simple gift inspired quite a movement of giving!

Before her death in 1999 at age ninety-one, Oseola McCarty had become famous, and that fact made her retirement years dramatically different from what her earlier life had been like. Major newspapers and magazines featured articles on her. She received the Presidential Citizens Medal, an honorary doctorate degree from Harvard University, a medal from UNESCO, and more than three hundred various awards. She was even featured on a Barbara Walters television special. While Oseola seemed to appreciate the attention and travel that her newly found fame bought her, she complained, "I don't want to be put up on a pedestal. I want to stay right here on the ground."[15] Oseola shared her philosophy in a book called *Simple Wisdom for Rich Living*. In his review of the book, Louis Carlozo of the *Chicago Tribune* said, "McCarty's wisdom is…reminiscent of a cross between *The Wealthy Barber* and Mother Teresa's *A Simple Path*. Seeds of wisdom spill from the pages, and any reader prudent enough to plant them could find themselves laying the bed for a similarly rich life."[16]

Oseola McCarty patiently planted one seed of kindness at a time over a period of seventy years. The garden of giving that she inspired continues to bloom today, and her legacy will bear seeds for years to come.

DON'T JUDGE
EACH DAY
BY THE
HARVEST
YOU REAP
BUT BY
THE SEEDS
YOU PLANT.

ROBERT LOUIS STEVENSON

SCATTERING JOY
WHEN IT'S NOT EASY

Nothing in life is to be feared.
It is only to be understood.

Marie Curie

When everything is all hunky-dory, we are easily filled with a giving spirit. When life seems to be in tune for us, nothing is more natural than wanting to share with others. But what about the times we feel out of sorts or, worse yet, feel that life is treating us unfairly?

It's also natural to want to share joy with people we are close to—with family members, with friends, and with people who have been kind to us. Such reciprocal kindness comes easily, but showing kindness to people who aren't warm, outgoing, or fair

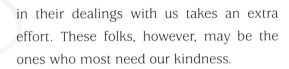

in their dealings with us takes an extra effort. These folks, however, may be the ones who most need our kindness.

When I was teaching, I had a troubling experience with one of the school secretaries. It may have been a minor incident, but it took me by surprise and shook me up. I had always taken pride in the fact that I could get along with almost anyone. I felt I could pretty easily understand and accept differing viewpoints and perspectives.

I was in my classroom one morning with a room full of students when a secretary I'll call Belinda buzzed me on the intercom. She asked whether a certain student in my class was available, and I told her that he wasn't present. After she hung up, I pulled out the daily attendance sheet and noticed that his name was listed as an absentee that day. I figured Belinda must not have noticed this, and if someone was looking for my student, I'd better alert her to the fact that he hadn't come to school at all that day. When I buzzed Belinda back with the information, she was very abrupt with me, leaving me a little red-faced since my whole class overheard the brief exchange. After class was over, I stopped by the office in an effort to smooth things over.

When I opened the office door, Belinda practically crawled over the reception counter. (At least it seemed like that to me!) She was pointing her finger at me, saying, "Don't you *ever* correct me like that, especially in front of your students!" She continued, "Of course I knew he was on the absentee list"—and was I supposed to have known that?—"and we think he may be skipping school. I was checking to see if he might have shown up."

I was dumbstruck. Feeling wrongly accused when I had only tried to be helpful, I was completely flustered. But as I often do in such circumstances, I cowered to her ranting, apologized, and walked out of the office with my tail between my legs. You see, for me, it's always afterward that I think of my comeback. I tend to absorb things rather than respond, and this was one time I regretted doing so. *I should have stood my ground,* I thought. *I should have told her she was acting like a maniac! I should have pointed my finger right back at her and put her in her place!* But instead I just felt hurt. I thought she knew me better than to assume I was trying to put her down. I decided I'd have to show Belinda just how wrong she was.

When I went home that night, I told my husband about Belinda's shocking action and how hurt and angry that small incident had left me. Being a counselor by profession, he had the good sense to set me straight.

"Kathy, don't you see that it wasn't you that she was reacting to? She must have either been having a terrible day, or it's possible that she is just a very unhappy person."

LOVE
YOUR NEIGHBOR
AS YOURSELF.
MATTHEW 22:39 (NIV)

As I thought about this over the next several days, I came to believe that Belinda must indeed be very dissatisfied with her life. I noticed that she rarely smiled and definitely seemed to have a chip on her shoulder. I started to feel badly for her even though she had remained cold and distant after our incident. My need for revenge began turning into a different kind of need. I decided that the better way for me to show her who I was and turn her disapproval of me into approval was to extend some kindness to her. Besides, she really seemed to need it.

> ## WHAT DO WE LIVE FOR, IF NOT TO MAKE LIFE LESS DIFFICULT FOR EACH OTHER?
> GEORGE ELIOT

While my motivation may have been self-serving, I learned during this process how much I could gain by looking past personal differences. At some point I finally felt that I had gained Belinda's trust as a friend. During my campaign for revenge, I had been softened as I saw Belinda as the vulnerable person she really was. Not only was I able to forgive, but I also found some qualities in my new friend that made me a better friend myself. Our relationship became a truly rewarding one for me—and, by the way, it doesn't hurt to have school secretaries as friends when you teach!

Differences often separate us from other people, and we miss out on what could be rewarding relationships. Just as we often fear things that we don't understand, the same can be true about people. Whether they are from other cultures, religions, political beliefs, or moral orientations, our unfounded fears can prevent any real understanding of each other.

This observation reminds me of an amazing story I came across on a YouTube link a friend e-mailed me.[17] (Isn't that how we find out about everything these days?). The clip features two very unlikely costars and offers a lesson about looking past differences.

One day Mr. and Mrs. Collito, an older couple living in Massachusetts, noticed a stray kitten in their backyard. Realizing that the kitten could only be a few months old, the couple feared for its safety. The next day, however, they noticed a crow that seemed to be chasing the small cat. Upon closer observation, though, they noticed that these two natural enemies seemed to be companions of sorts. As the Collitos watched, they were amazed to see that the crow was picking worms and bugs from the ground and feeding them to the hungry kitten! As hard as it was to fathom, this crow seemed to have adopted the homeless kitty!

They called the local veterinarian to ask for advice. Doubting their story, he urged them to document their observations. So, for eight months, the couple filmed the unlikely duo. The video shows the crow protecting and nurturing the kitten day after day, even crowing his cautionary calls when the cat tried to cross the road. When the Collitos started offering food to the duo, they would share it, taking turns with the bounty.

At some point, the kitten began trusting the couple and spending nights in their home, but each morning the crow would come calling at the kitchen window and beckon its friend to come and play.

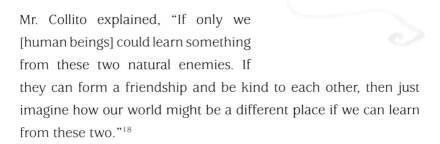

Mr. Collito explained, "If only we [human beings] could learn something from these two natural enemies. If they can form a friendship and be kind to each other, then just imagine how our world might be a different place if we can learn from these two."[18]

You can link to the video clip of these unlikely friends at:
scatterjoy.com.

Something to Think About:

How open are you to forming relationships with those who are different from you? What can you do to overcome whatever barriers may be holding you back?

How
beautiful
a day can be
when kindness
touches it.

G. Elliston

RANDOM ACTS OF KINDNESS

Wherever there is a human being,
there is an opportunity for kindness.
Seneca

Practice random kindness and senseless acts of beauty.

Read what Wikipedia says:

> A random act of kindness is a purportedly selfless act performed by a person or persons wishing to either assist or cheer up an individual or, in some cases, even an animal. There will generally be no reason other than to make people smile, or be happier. Either spontaneous or planned in advance, random acts of kindness are encouraged by various communities. An oft-cited example of a random act of kindness is, when paying the toll at a toll booth on a highway, to pay the toll for the vehicle behind you as well.[19]

The phrase *Practice random kindness and senseless acts of beauty* may have been coined by peace activist Anne Herbert. Herbert says she wrote it on a placemat at a Sausalito restaurant in 1982 or 1983.[20] I remember the first time I heard this now widely recognized phrase. *What a nice message*, I thought, *and so beautifully said!*

After hearing about some random kindnesses, I decided I'd better get with the program. While I love the random nature of this concept, I thought I'd get in the groove with a few premeditated acts. Then, I figured, I'd be more aware as random opportunities presented themselves. And I thought the idea of paying the toll for a car behind me was the best place to start. Perfect! What fun this would be! I decided that a two-dollar toll had more bang than a measly fifty-cent one, so on the way home from a short trip, I picked out a toll booth along the expressway, and had my four dollars all ready—two for me and two for that lucky car behind me....

Except that, much to my chagrin, not only was there no car behind me as I approached the toll booth, but I seemed to be the lone car on the highway that day. This was no fun! There was not a single car in sight. I'd imagined I'd be able to at least catch a glimpse of my "lottery winner" in the rear-view mirror as I pulled away after paying. Never even seeing my recipient was a bit too random for me!

So, when I paid my two dollars to the obviously bored toll taker, I explained, "I'd intended to pay the toll for the car behind me to surprise someone, but since I don't see any, I'd like you to have this two dollars so you can treat yourself to a cup of coffee on me." The toll taker's face broke into a huge smile, and with a "Thank you so much, honey!" she let out a great big belly laugh. As I pulled away, her laughter still echoed in my ears and my heart. With that little two-buck investment, I had just bought myself a high that would carry me through my day. In fact, every time I think of that woman's laughter, I get a return on that investment.

Something to Think About:

Look at the Random Acts of Kindness list on this page and choose one act of kindness to perform today.

RANDOM ACTS OF KINDNESS

There are endless ways to commit Random Acts of Kindness. Here are some of my favorite ideas:

- Take a flower to a friend... for no special reason. Tie it with a ribbon or place it in a pretty bud vase.

- Make or buy some musical windchimes and place them where all can enjoy.

- Never let a loving thought go unspoken.

- Leave your small change for a worthy charity when you're at the cash register.

- Send upbeat e-mail messages!

- Clip articles of interest and funny stories and surprise someone by sending them through the mail.

- Place pennies on the sidewalk with a chalk-written "Make a wish today."

- Leave unused coupons on the appropriate shelf in the supermarket for the next person to use.

- Do the dishes at home or at the office even if it's not your turn.

THIS IS THE DAY
THE LORD
HAS MADE;
LET US
REJOICE
&
BE GLAD IN IT.

Psalm 118:24 (NIV)

THE JOY OF GRATITUDE

There are only two ways to live your life.
One is as though nothing is a miracle.
The other is as though everything
is a miracle.
Albert Einstein

We all know the tremendous feeling of gratitude we experience when we hear good news about something we've been worrying about. Whether it's as serious as a medical diagnosis, as life changing as getting a new job, or as important as selling a house, our natural response is thankfulness. We may even spontaneously offer a prayer of gratitude for this gift of good news.

But when it comes to the smaller blessings that surround us each and every day, we may be so busy or preoccupied with our worries and challenges that we overlook all that is going well for us.

And I have found that nothing I have found can turn negative thoughts into a positive outlook faster than the practice of gratitude. That's why I try to make this practice a part of my daily morning ritual, although it can be transformative anytime,

especially when I am starting to feel sorry for myself. Gratitude takes my "woe is me" feeling and turns it right on its head.

Sometimes, for instance, I feel myself stuck or overwhelmed in work. Then I remember just how fortunate I am to *have* work when many people are either without jobs or struggling to make ends meet. At other times, I feel stressed because of family issues or relationship pressures. Once again I pause to remember just how blessed I am to have a loving husband, wonderful kids, a dear mother, and precious friends and family members when many individuals are very alone in this world.

Then there are those times when I am hard on myself, when I get down on myself and wish I'd lose a few pounds or work out harder and more consistently. Then I realize how blessed I am to have my health, and I remind myself that I need to accept and appreciate who I am, knowing I can make healthy choices for myself anytime.

Scientific studies have confirmed that gratitude plays an important role in a person's sense of well-being. Philosophers and spiritual teachers throughout history have celebrated gratitude, and the world's major religions value it as a beneficial emotional state that helps to promote kindness.

Dr. Michael McCullough of Southern Methodist University and Dr. Robert Emmons of the University of California at Davis conducted a research project on gratitude and thanksgiving.[21] Three groups of participants were asked to keep daily diaries. Group 1 simply recorded the events that occurred each day, Group 2 kept track of the unpleasant experiences of each day, and Group 3 made a daily list of the things for which they were grateful. Not surprisingly, the results indicated that Group 3 reported higher levels of alertness, enthusiasm, determination, optimism, and energy. Members of Group 3 also experienced less stress and depression; they were more likely to help others; and they made significant progress toward their personal goals. Clearly, gratitude encourages a cycle of kindness… and is therefore a perfect way to scatter joy!

THERE IS NO ONE LUCKIER THAN HE WHO THINKS HIMSELF SO.

GERMAN PROVERB

If the results of this study aren't enough motivation for you to want to develop an attitude of gratitude, I don't know what you need! That said, practice will help you make gratitude a healthy habit.

Whether you make some time to give thanks each morning, every evening, or in the middle of your day is up to you. Maybe a weekly or monthly date to devote some time to thanksgiving suits you better. One day you may even find yourself shifting to a "gratitude attitude" whenever you catch yourself in a downward "woe is me" spiral.

Once you make gratitude a habit, your brain will become more aware and in tune with all of the wonderful things happening in your life, where before you might not have even given them a second thought.

Something to Think About:

What are you especially grateful for today? Why does that make you grateful?

An Exercise in Gratitude

Ask yourself these questions:

- What is my greatest source of joy at this time in my life?

- What am I most looking forward to in my life?

- What am I most committed to in my life right now?

- What one thing can I do today that will bring me joy?

- What one thing can I do for someone else today to scatter joy?

Practicing gratitude will probably inspire you to express your gratitude to others or to give thanks in prayer. Whether you share your thanks verbally, on paper, or by your actions, you will taste the joy of letting others know that their kindness, support, or presence in your life makes a difference. In fact, your own joyful gratitude will increase as you scatter it to others.

GRATITUDE PRAYERS

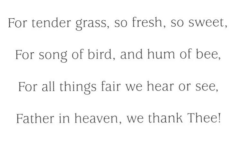

For flowers that bloom about our feet,

For tender grass, so fresh, so sweet,

For song of bird, and hum of bee,

For all things fair we hear or see,

Father in heaven, we thank Thee!

For blue of stream and blue of sky,

For pleasant shade of branches high,

For fragrant air and cooling breeze,

For beauty of the blooming trees,

Father in heaven, we thank Thee!

Author Unknown

The Blessing of Unanswered Prayers

I asked for strength that I might achieve;
I was made weak that I might learn humbly to obey.

I asked for health that I might do greater things;
I was given infirmity that I might do better things.

I asked for riches that I might be happy;
I was given poverty that I might be wise.

I asked for power that I might have the praise of men;
I was given weakness that I might feel the need of God.

I asked for all things that I might enjoy life;
I was given life that I might enjoy all things.

I got nothing that I had asked for
but everything that I had hoped for.

Almost despite myself my unspoken prayers were answered;
I am, among all men, most richly blessed.

Prayer of an Unknown Confederate Soldier

SANDIE ANDERSEN

SCATTER JOY SPOTLIGHT

I've seen and met angels wearing the disguise of ordinary people living ordinary lives.   Tracy Chapman.

Sandie Andersen works at a Starbucks in Tacoma, Washington. This fifty-one-year-old barista is known for serving friendly small talk to her customers along with their tall mocha lattes and chai teas.

One morning, one of Sandie's regular customers stopped in for her daily dose of caffeine and conversation. But that day customer Annamarie Ausnes seemed quieter than usual when she ordered her usual "short drip, double cupped" java jolt.[22] The barista picked up on this immediately and asked if something was wrong. The two women had known each other casually for the three years that Annamarie had been stopping by this Starbucks. But during their morning small-talk sessions, Annamarie had never mentioned the kidney disease that she had been dealing with for nearly twenty years. Her disorder causes complications that lead to eventual kidney failure.[23] Annamarie's health had suddenly begun to decline, and she had just learned that her only option was a transplant. Since her husband and son weren't matches, she was facing a long wait on a transplant list.

When Annamarie told her the sad news, Sandie's response was instantaneous. "I'm going to get tested," she said.[24] And get tested she did. Not only did her blood type match, but so did the results of all the other tests. Sandie's kidney could indeed be a match for Annamarie.

After the successful surgery, both women are expected to be fine. Annemarie says she found her guardian angel in this casual acquaintance. "We had a friendship, but now that I have a part of Sandie, I'm family."[25]

And Sandie, who had previously done missionary work in Mexico and hurricane relief work in New Orleans, said her kidney donation should not be viewed as heroic. People should give freely of themselves, and more of them do than get noticed. As for losing her kidney, Sandie said, "I just felt in my heart it was the right thing to do."[26]

How better to scatter joy than by giving the gift of life to another!

Live life
in full
bloom.

CREATE A LIFE YOU LOVE

Life isn't about finding yourself.
Life is about creating yourself.

George Bernard Shaw

It's up to you. You have the power to not only attract

the things you want in life, but to help create them. While this is an

empowering idea, it can be daunting at the same time. First, you

need clarity in order to envision the life you desire. Second, you

need the courage to create your own path. Then with some honest

soul searching, consistent hard work, focused determination, and

prayer for guidance, you can make the choices you need in order

to live the life you envision.

Sure, we will always be dealing with circumstances beyond our

control. We are born into a way of life that helps set our course, and no matter what changes we make to affect our future, we will always encounter opposing forces. The key is to not settle for circumstances that someone else hands you if they don't feel right for you.

We also need to remember that we aren't in charge of the universe. That job is already taken! But it is up to us to make wise choices in life, and if we don't make 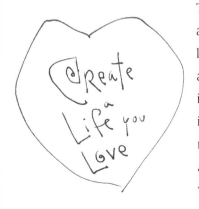 those choices for ourselves, we can be sure that others will make them for us. While our tendency may be to please the people in our lives, especially those people we love and respect, our efforts to live according to what others may think best for us will not bring fulfillment in life. Each one of us has been blessed with special talents, desires, needs, and dreams, and it takes real courage to stay true to them. But when we do, we are able to share—out of our fullness—more of our joy and gifts with others.

•   •   •

To create a rich and balanced life, we need to address each of the four dimensions of our lives: the spiritual, the physical, the emotional, and the intellectual. Identifying what's important to us in each of these four areas is our first and most important step. Setting realistic goals and priorities is the next one. And making them happen, adjusting along the way, completes the ongoing, lifelong process.

For me, identifying what I want has always been challenging. Once I get clarity, it becomes much easier for me to follow through. We all know the saying, "Be careful what you ask for because you might just get it." Sometimes we get what we ask for, and it turns out to be not at all what we expected or even want anymore. But even if you do find yourself unhappy with a decision you've made, it is never too late to change it. You may need to take a different path than you first might have, but the important thing is to take action. You can correct your course later. We all do it.

Going through the life-changing experience of divorce led me to search for deeper meaning, personal fulfillment, and creative freedom, somehow all packaged in such a way that I could support myself and my children. I was scared and stymied. How would I ever find my way? Answers certainly didn't come overnight, nor were they ever neatly packaged with a set of instructions, but the answers did come to me... one piece at a time.

When I am lost in my jumbled thoughts and unsure what direction to take, I find that prayer has a calming effect on me. I realize I am  not alone on my journey. But without a map, I know it is up to me to discover my own truths. I look for tools that may help me identify or pinpoint answers that are right for me.

One of the most useful tools in helping me find my path was the book, still popular today, *What Color Is Your Parachute?*

A Practical Manual for Job-Hunters and Career-Changers by Richard Nelson Bolles.[27] Visually appealing and brimming with information and exercises, this manual is user-friendly and not the least bit intimidating. It was just what I needed!

The one exercise that still sticks out in my mind helped me identify those accomplishments in my life that had given me the greatest satisfaction, enjoyment, and fulfillment. The next step was identifying the skills that I used in each of these experiences. Once I did that, I was excited to see some ways I could use my skills that would be fulfilling!

As I was trying to recall this exercise, I decided to see if I could locate on my crowded bookshelves the very book I had used. To my surprise, I found my copy of the 1985 edition of *What Color Is Your Parachute?* (It sometimes pays to be a pack rat!) Even more fun was discovering the notes I had written in the margins those many years ago.

OTHER PEOPLE WOULD CALL IT **WORK.** BUT I'M JUST **PLAYING** VERY HARD.

JACK LEVOR LARSON

Those notes provided me with a nifty little time capsule. Looking back to when I completed this exercise, I marvel at how closely my findings have been reflected in my life and work today, some twenty-three years later! As an artist and small business owner, I use most of those skills I identified as I do the work I love.

I believe that exercises like the one I just described can help illuminate all aspects of our life. When we see patterns in the things that have been rewarding and pleasing, we can take cues that will help determine the course we'd like to take for our spiritual, physical, emotional, and intellectual growth—and for joy. Paying close attention to those things that bring us joy is critical to creating a life that we love.

I can, for instance, clearly see in my son, Ben, a pattern that has been evident throughout his life. His love for anything musical was obvious from an early age.

THE MAN WHO WAS BORN WITH A TALENT WHICH HE IS MEANT TO USE FINDS HIS GREATEST HAPPINESS IN USING IT.

GOETHE

He'd spend hours on Christmas mornings with any musical gifts—ranging from a mini-keyboard and a plastic record player to a toy drum machine and even a kazoo. Ben would be instantly smitten! Paying little to no attention to the shiny new trucks or baseballs, Ben always preferred to have a guitar in hand. Today, in his mid-twenties, he plays in a band and enjoys writing and composing songs as well. Music is his joy.

Sometimes, we instinctively know what is right for us. At other times, though, we may need to do some work to uncover these truths.

The path we are called to take may be there waiting for us. But at other times we may need to forge our own path.

AND THE DAY CAME
WHEN THE RISK
TO REMAIN
TIGHT IN A BUD
WAS MORE
PAINFUL THAN
THE RISK IT TOOK
TO
BLOSSOM.

ANAIS NIN

Either way, working toward living a life we love is worth the effort. Using our talents and gifts in a way that brings us joy is not only our right, but also our responsibility. And when we live a life of joy, we are able to share that joy with those around us. Living a fulfilling life allows us to give from our fullness. And, after all, giving with a heart full of gratitude and joy is the only way to give.

Something to Think About:

Is the life you are living the life that wants to live in you?

(Paraphrase of a quote by Parker Palmer)

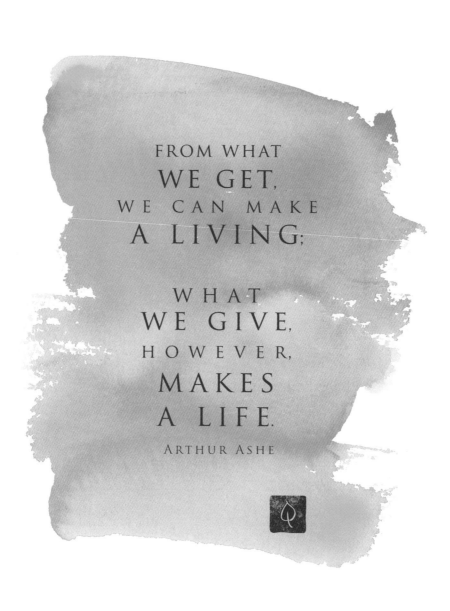

FROM WHAT
WE GET,
WE CAN MAKE
A LIVING;

WHAT
WE GIVE,
HOWEVER,
MAKES
A LIFE.

ARTHUR ASHE

A NEVER-ENDING PROCESS

Life is, for most of us,
a continuous process of getting used to
things we hadn't expected. Martha Lupton

Creating the life you love will be an ongoing process. Circumstances in life are always changing. And, although we inherently stay the same inside, we need to adapt to our world as it changes, constantly altering our perspective to the sun.

Life is change, and change (even good change) can be difficult and even painful. If we don't stay flexible and adapt, we will hurt ourselves and limit our growth.

Also keep in mind that what's right for us in our twenties may not fit when we are in our forties. As we learn and grow, we need to shed our skin in order to make room for the new things in life. Sometimes these new things will call for subtle changes; sometimes the necessary changes will be quite radical.

Keeping your life in tune takes vigilance, but it doesn't have to feel like work.

We are wise to be open to the happy surprises that come our way—and open to the ways those surprises can redirect our paths. We are also wise to choose to adjust to circumstances that we wouldn't choose for ourselves, circumstances that may be beyond our control regardless of our best efforts.

Lord,
grant me
the
serenity
to accept
the things I cannot
change,
the courage to
change the things I can,
and the wisdom
to know
the difference.

St. Francis of Assisi

At this point in my life, I am again facing changes in both my professional and personal life that I didn't necessarily plan on. I have no doubt, however, that these changes will bring new opportunities for me to grow and learn. Even though I am once again out of my comfort zone, I look forward to seeing what new threads I'll be adding to this rich tapestry of life I am weaving.

MY HOPE STILL IS
TO LEAVE THE WORLD
A LITTLE BIT BETTER
THAN WHEN I GOT HERE.

JIM HENSON

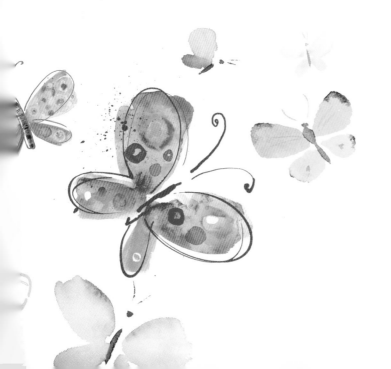

SCATTERING JOY AT WORK: KATHY DAVIS STUDIOS

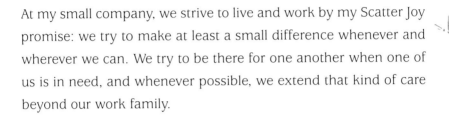

At my small company, we strive to live and work by my Scatter Joy promise: we try to make at least a small difference whenever and wherever we can. We try to be there for one another when one of us is in need, and whenever possible, we extend that kind of care beyond our work family.

The list of worthy charitable organizations and programs is endless. Here are a few that we have worked with and their Web addresses where you can learn more about them.

- Toys for Tots (*toysfortots.org*)
- Canned food drives for local food cupboards
- Operation Christmas Child (*samaritanspurse.org*)
- Katrina trip (company-sponsored travel and paid time off)
  - Presbyterian Disaster Assistance (*pcusa.org*)
  - Associations for Community Organizations for Reform Now (*acorn.org*)
  - Starbucks Make Your Mark (*starbucks.com*)
- Home building in Mexico: Amor Ministries (*amor.org*)
- Dress for Success, an organization that offers low-income women interview clothes, career-development tips, and confidence boost (*dressforsuccess.org*)

- Lance Armstrong Foundation (*livestrong.com/visit-laf/*)
  Visit Flowerbud.com to purchase the Livestrong Bicyclette Bouquet. A portion of the proceeds is given to the Lance Armstrong Foundation.
- Walk-a-thons
- Mentoring and internship programs
- Product donations (schools, raffles, art auctions)
  - "If the Shoe Fits" Auction & Fundraiser: The Center for Patient Partnerships
    (*cppiftheshoefits.org*)
- Donations of proceeds
  - Children's Charity
    Sunshine Foundation (*sunshinefoundation.org*)
  - Animal Services Buddy Dog Humane Society
    (*buddydoghs.com*)
  - Help for the Homeless
    National Interfaith Hospitality Network (*www.nihn.org*)
  - Wildflower Preservation
    Lady Bird Johnson Wildflower Center (*wildflower.org*)

For more information and additional stories, visit kdstudio.blogspot. com. In particular, don't miss KDS president John Mavrakis's story "What If" in the December 2007 post.

Many companies, both large and small, have wonderful programs and employee incentives for helping others. Please share some of your stories with me at scatterjoy.com.

Acknowledgments

All of the stories, photos, tidbits, and quotes in this book were collected over time, contributed by family, friends, acquaintances and fellow employees. We have diligently strived to properly acknowledge each and every person, place, and source, though in some cases we found it to be an undertaking beyond our abilities. To each contributor and/or author, we wish to express our sincere thanks and, where necessary, our sincere apologies.

Unless otherwise noted, all of the art and photographs in this book are either the property of Kathy Davis Studios or taken from the personal collection of Kathy Davis. Our sincere thanks to both Peter Walts and Katie Davis for sharing their photographic skills in the many photos that grace the pages of this book.

Endnotes

1 Pauline Rose Clance and Suzanne Imes, "The Imposter Phenomenon in High Achieving Women: Dynamics and Therapeutic Intervention," Georgia State University, Psycotherapy Theory Research and Practice, Volume 15, #3, http://www2.gsu.edu/ ~ wwwaow/resources/ip_high_achieving_women.pdf,Fall 1978.

2 *World Book Dictionary* (CR-ROM), Mac, (World Book, Inc., 2005).

3 Sue Bender, *Plain and Simple: A Woman's Journey to the Amish* (New York: HarperOne, 1991).

4 Véronique Vienne, *The Art of Doing Nothing: Simple Ways to Make Time for Yourself* (Clarkson Potter, 1998).

5 Amy E. Dean, *Peace of Mind: Daily Meditations for Easing Stress* (New York: Bantam, 1995).

6 Experience Bermuda, "What Makes Johnny Wave?," http://experience-bermuda.com/sightseeing/friendliest-man.html.

7 Wikipedia, "Johnny Barnes," http://en.wikipedia.org/wiki/johnny_barnes.

8 Devore Community Swimming Pool Association, "Maisie's Community Swimming Pool," http://www.maisiespool.com/maisiesstory.html, 16 September 2008.

9 Steve Hartman, CBS News, "Weeding By Example," http://www.cbsnews.com/stories//2007/08/24/assignment_america/main3202058.shtml?source=search_story, 24 August 2007.

10 Marilyn Elias, *USA Today,* "Never too young to help out," http://www.usatoday.com/news/nation/2007-08-15-neworleans-teen_n.htm,5 September 2008.

11 Hartman.

12 Anonymous.

13 Anonymous.

14 Rick Bragg, *The New York Times,* "Oseola McCarty, 91, Washerwoman with a Heart of Gold," http://www.mishalov.com/McCarty.html, 28 September 1999.

15 Tolitha Clark, Mississippi Writers and Musicians, "Oseola McCarty," http://www.mswritersandmusicians.com/writers/oseola-mccarty.html, 1999.

16 Louis R. Carlozo, "Oseola McCarty's Simple Wisdom for Rich Living: Words from the Laundress Whose $150,000 Scholarship Gift Inspired the Nation" http://www.generousgiving.org/book_reviews/display.asp?id=13.

17 Wally and Ann Collito, Miracle Pets, "Crow and Kitten Are Friends," http://www.youtube.com/watch?v=1JiJzqXxgxo, 1999.

18 Collito.

19 Wikipedia, "Random Act of Kindness," http://en.wikipedia.org/wiki/Random_act_of_kindness.

20 Wikipedia, "Random Act of Kindness."

21 ACF Newsource, "Gratitude Theory," http://www.acfnewsource.org/religion/gratitude_theory.html, 31 December 2006.

22 William Yardley, *The New York Times,* "A Donor Match Over Small Talk and Coffee," http://www.nytimes.com/2008/03/04/us/04barista.html, 4 March 2008.

23 Cherie Black, *Seattle Post-Intelligencer,* "Starbucks barista donates kidney to one of her regulars," http://seattlepi.nwsource.com/health/354672_starbuckskidney12.html, 12 March 2008.

24 Yardley.

25 Mike Celizic, *The Today Show,* "Would You Like a Kidney with That?," http://today.msnbc.msn.com/id/23917493/, 2 April 2008.

26 Celizic.

27 Richard Nelson Bolles, *What Color Is Your Parachute? A Practical Manual for Job Hunters and Career Changers* (California: Ten Speed Press, 2007).

Notes